Journeys through Vanishing Worlds

Published and Forthcoming by New Academia Publishing

Russian History and Culture

THE INNER ADVERSARY: The Struggle against Philistinism as the Moral Mission of the Russian Intelligentsia, by Timo Vihavainen

RUSSIAN FUTURISM: A History, by Vladimir Markov

WORDS IN REVOLUTION: Russian Futurist Manifestoes 1912-1928, A. Lawton and H. Eagle, eds., trs.

IMAGING RUSSIA 2000: Film and Facts, by Anna Lawton

BEFORE THE FALL: Soviet Cinema in the Gorbachev Years, by Anna Lawton

RED ATTACK WHITE RESISTANCE: Civil War in South Russia, 1918, by Peter Kenez

RED ADVANCE WHITE DEFEAT: Civil War in South Russia, 1919-1920, by Peter Kenez

REMEMBERING UTOPIA: The Culture of Everyday Life in Socialist Yugoslavia Breda Luthar and Marusa Pušnik, eds.

THE SOVIETIZATION OF EASTERN EUROPE: New Perspectives, Balázs Apor, Péter Apor and E. A. Rees, eds.

History / International Affairs

TURKEY'S MODERNIZATION: Refugees from Nazism and Atatürk's Vision by Arnold Reisman

GOD, GREED, AND GENOCIDE: The Holocaust through the Centuries by Arthur Grenke

NATIONALISM, HISTORIOGRAPHY AND THE (RE)CONSTRUCTION OF THE PAST, Edited by Claire Norton

AN ARCHITECT OF DEMOCRACY: Building a Mosaic of Peace by James Robert Huntley, Foreword by Brent Scowcroft. (Memoirs and Occasional Papers, Association for Diplomatic Studies and Training)

ECHOES OF A DISTANT CLARION: Recollections of a Diplomat and Soldier, by John G. Kormann (Memoirs and Occasional Papers, Association for Diplomatic Studies and Training)

PETER STRICKLAND: New London Shipmaster, Boston Merchant, First Consul to Senegal, by Stephen H. Grant (ADST-DACOR Diplomats and Diplomacy Book)

Scarith Books (fiction / memoirs)

ON THE WAY TO RED SQUARE, by Julieta Almeida Rodrigues

FROM WARSAW TO WHEREVER, by Zygmunt Nagorski

THROUGH DARK DAYS AND WHITE NIGHTS, by Naomi F. Collins

PETS OF THE GREAT DICTATORS & Other Works, by Sabrina P. Ramet

Journeys through Vanishing Worlds

Abraham Brumberg

 An imprint of New Academia Publishing
Washington, DC

Copyright © 2007 by Abraham Brumberg

SCARITH/New Academia Publishing, 2007

All rights reserved. No part of this book may be reproduced or transmitted in any form or by any means, electronic or mechanical, including photocopying, recording, or by any information storage and retrieval system.

Printed in the United States of America

Library of Congress Control Number: 2007936715
ISBN 978-0-9794488-7-4 paperback (alk. paper)

 An imprint of New Academia Publishing
P.O. Box 24720, Washington, DC 20038-7420

 info@newacademia.com
www.newacademia.com

Contents

Introduction ix

1. Warsaw-Tel Aviv-Warsaw 1
Two Bundists in Tel Aviv. Hebrew, Yiddish, Polish. Back to Warsaw. The Medem Sanatorium, a world unto itself. The child as Insider and Outsider.

2. Growing up a socialist 9
The sanatorium as utopia. mir kumen on. How I became class conscious. Socialism vs. anti-Semitism. The Yiddish school and other organizations. The Bund victorious.

3. September 1939: from Warsaw to Vilna. 19
War tremors. Gymnazjum and war. Farewell, Warsaw. mishpokhedikayt. oyf gots barot. From Luniniec to Lunin. The Red Army takes over. Vilna in our dreams.

4. Vilna 1939-1941 29
A world turned topsy-turvy. The charms of Vilna. Long live khaver Stalin! A curious birthday. My father goes into hiding. On the move again.

5. The Great Adventure, part one. 43
To Moscow. A Guided Tour. By Train Through Siberia. A Whiff of Birobidjan. Farewell Russia!

6. The Great Adventure, part two.   51

A Fairy Tale Called Japan. The Delights of Kobe. Yokohama and the US Consulate. The Asama Maru. My First Seduction. America!

7. Los Angeles, 1941-1942   59

The Bund in the New World. A Tempting Offer. So How do You Like this Country? Into Long Pants. Conversing with the Natives. Yiddish Under the Palms. A Personal Holocaust. Back to Los Angeles. Wowing Them.

    77

8. Tumultuous Teens

The Bronx. Avrom Reizin. A European Amongst Americans. A Communist Teacher. Rebel with Causes. The Two Brothers Weinreich. Honor The Memory. Life Goes On...

9. The Army and Americanization   93

Graduation and Citizenship. Army Chaos. Loneliness. Ominous Rumors. Fort Knox Hospital. Jim Crow. Basic Training Manqué.

Photo Gallery   109

10. CCNY and All That   127

Christmas and Chanukah. Politics and student life. Commemorating the Warsaw Ghetto. Academic discoveries. Resign, Brumberg, resign! Singing and Skiing. Professional presentiments.

11. Lev Davidovich   139

A seminal figure. My first Trotskyite. Cannon and Shachtman. Trotsky at CCNY. Trotsky, Wittfogel, Spies. Browder vs. Shachtman.

12. Into Sovietology   155

The approaching future. Jewish non-Jews. Soviet studies. Hot war, cold war. Kak skazat' po-russki. Coded messages. Conventional Courses. Bertram D. Wolfe. My career begins.

13. Sovietology Engagement   167

Birth of a Journal. Scribblers and Gumshoes. What's in a Name? A Serious Rift. Same or Different? Straight But Not Narrow. Have Journal Will Travel. Dramatis Personae. The Social Democratic Option.

14. Poland Again   181

National Culture. Friends, Colleagues. The Eternal Wanderer. Poles Apart. In the Shadow of Solidarity. Despair and Hope. The Dissipation of a Dream.

15. Russia Again   191

The Priviligentsia... Workers versus Workers? Dissent and Samizdat. A soupçon of liberalism. Shifting Patterns. Three Portraits.

16. Envoi   203

Notes   207

Introduction

This book, in gestation for nearly three years, is neither a travelogue nor, strictly speaking, a memoir, though it fuses ingredients from both these genres. Rather, it is an attempt to make sense out of a peripatetic life that took me, by a bizarre concatenation of circumstances, from Palestine, where I happened to be born, to Poland, where by all rights I should have been born, thence, after several years in and around Warsaw, proceeding eastwards across wartorn Poland before reaching Vilna in early September 1939 and then later the United States.

Thus, only two months past my thirteenth birthday, I had already departed from two of the "worlds" mentioned in the book's title, the word "world" used in both a geographic and cultural sense. In Palestine, the first world, my parents and I lived in a modest shack near the beach in Tel Aviv, and my language was Hebrew, my Yiddish-speaking parents' concession to acculturation. My father came home every evening from his main job digging ditches in the growing Tel Aviv harbor, or from his second job attending to a small "library on wheels," mostly Yiddish titles and none of them more dog-eared, my father would later recollect, than the Yiddish version of *Oliver Twist*.

This idyll could not last long. In the late 1920s Palestine was swept by a series of anti-Jewish riots. Since my father had never been a Zionist but a Bundist, rejecting the notion of a Jewish state in favor of a socialist revolution for all humankind, and a belief that Yiddish was the *lingua franca* of all East European Jews, he was happy to accept the offer of a job as a director of a Bundist-run children's sanatorium near Warsaw.

Thus I was propelled into different worlds, all interconnected in one way or another, each, however, marked by discrete boundaries. In my Poland, life from childhood to the teens revolved around the Jewish socialist organization Bund and its institutions for children and youth. When war forced us to leave, our trek eastward – commencing a few days after the war broke out on September 1, 1939 – took us through yet another world of small villages and *shtetlekh*, small towns inhabited by Jewish small artisans and traders and local Polish, Belorussian or Ukrainian peasants. Eventually we reached the Polish-Lithuanian city of Vilna, whose Jewish population of about 60,000 constituted a distinct cultural milieu; soon after our arrival, it was incorporated into the Soviet Union.

My experience of this kaleidoscope of worlds I journeyed through – Warsaw, Vilna, Moscow, and then through Kobe and Yokohama to Los Angeles, New York and beyond – typical, if you will, of a twentieth-century Wandering Jew – was steeped in excitement. Gradually, however, the brevity of my sojourns in each became more apparent, and the price paid in unhappiness and broken dreams grew commensurately. Learning a new language – Polish, Russian, English, even a bit of Lithuanian – was an adventure in itself, often with long-term consequences: my Polish today is far better than my childhood Polish. But too often no sooner had I mastered a new language than the world to which it introduced me vanished.

Even the language of most value during my professional career, Russian, has become somewhat superfluous. I learned it as a budding Sovietologist at Yale University. I relished it later on, when I edited *Problems of Communism*, a U.S. Information Agency-sponsored journal, and on trips to the Soviet Union or in conversations with Russians at home and in emigration. Yet not only has the world of Soviet dissent disappeared: the Soviet Union itself has ceased to exist. And since my connection with Russia always had a political link, a link now gone, my trips have become fewer and farther between and my use of the language, a language I love, has dwindled.

Yiddish is a more poignant example. I spoke Yiddish with family and friends, with adults and young people; I wrote poetry in Yiddish; I sang songs in Yiddish; I composed an operetta in Yiddish.

Today there is hardly a single person in Washington, where I live, with whom I can speak Yiddish. Its world – the secular culture of my Yiddish – has vanished.

Compulsion dictated nearly every stage of my early journey through vanishing worlds, often accompanied by fear and uncertainty. We had to leave Poland and go east to escape from the steadily advancing German army. From Vilna we moved east to find a haven from the Soviet dictatorship, making a brief, enchanting if tense stopover in Japan. Arrival in the United States in 1941 did not complete the restless search for more promising vistas, whether in Los Angeles, New York, or Washington. Nearly all these journeys took place under the heavy cloud of the Holocaust. Among its millions of victims were my mother's family in Treblinka, my father's mother in the Vilna ghetto and my aunt's family in the forests of Lithuania and death camps of Estonia.

Like many people, I proceeded in my life along a path more crooked than straightforward. I seriously considered the theater as a career, Yiddish theater in particular. I produced and performed on two recordings, one of Yiddish folk songs and another of Yiddish poetry, both tributes to a language and repertoire I love. But I knew the world of Yiddish was vanishing and theater without Yiddish held no attraction for me. I also produced a record, with balladeer Joe Glazer, called *My Darling Party Line: Irreverent Songs, Ballads, and Airs*, a spoof on Communist myths. The Sovietological world has proved to be ephemeral: how can you have Sovietology without the Soviet Union? But when I was considering professional choices, it seemed likely to remain intact for a good long while. So I stayed with it...

What remains of the many vanishing worlds that once engaged me so feverishly? Not much. The Bund is gone. So is the Poland I knew. Yiddish has virtually disappeared. Sovietology is a thing of the past. Indeed the Soviet Union is a thing of the past. It is a sad record. Yet in this new century, as I bring this chronicle to an end, I do it with some confidence, past experiences notwithstanding. I do it trusting that if the memory of those worlds survives, new journeys will take place – new journeys informed and perhaps inspired by the old ones. That, at any rate, is my hope.

As a rule, an author acknowledges his debt to his wife at the end of the book, in a somewhat ritualistic form. Not I. The first on my list of acknowledgements is unhesitatingly my wife, Josephine Woll, without whose hours of painstaking help and technical assistance this book would not have come into fruition.

There are many others who gave me valuable support, which I acknowledge with gratitude and warmth: in England, Lee Langley, Theo Richmond, Bernard Wasserstein, Avi Shlaim, Martin Smith, Hugh Denman and Ian Jack; in Ireland (now), Conor and Zhanna O'Clery; in the U.S., Raye Farr, Walter Laqueur, Irena Lasota, Samuel Kassow, Sol Goldstein, Peter and Penny Kenez, Steven Zipperstein, Marianne Szegedy-Maszak and Steven Xanakos, my sisters-in-law Diana Zurer and Judy Woll, and my children, Daniel and Maia. It is to them, to Jonathan and Laurie, and to my grandchildren Zoe, Max and Gabriel, that I dedicate this book.

1

WARSAW-TEL AVIV-WARSAW

Two Bundists in Tel Aviv. Hebrew, Yiddish, Polish. Back to Warsaw. The Medem Sanatorium, a world unto itself. The child as Insider and Outsider.

I came into the world on November 7, 1926, at the Hadassah Hospital in Tel Aviv. There was nothing peculiar about it, except that my parents were dedicated Bundists – members of the Jewish socialist party in Poland – and Tel Aviv was not exactly the place where Bundists raised their offspring but rather the destination and nesting place for dedicated (anti-Bundist) Zionists.

How my parents came to set foot in Palestine is one of those bizarre stories typical of twentieth-century European Jews, many of whom would often find themselves where they had least expected to be. Had my father had his choice, he would probably have continued to stay in Vilna or in the near-by small *shtetl* (town) of Świenciany, where a good part of his family resided. He might have gone on teaching in the local Yiddish *gimnazjum* (academic high school), and then departed in due course for Warsaw, with its large Bundist organization and plenty of opportunities for young energetic party members.

But this was not to be. In the early 1920s, Poland was swept by strikes and outbreaks of violence to which the police responded with massive arrests that made no distinctions between *bona fide* strikers and hooligans, let alone between socialists and communists. For my father, active in a left-wing student organization that included both socialists and communists, the ground began to shake under his feet. On the advice of fellow Bundists, he went underground and then decided to flee abroad.

To this day I rue my failure to ask him about the details of his escape, which apparently had its share of exciting features, including donning a false beard, obtaining a false passport, departing for Danzig (Gdansk) under his new name (and new guise) and then boarding a train to Berlin. In the German capital, the local social democratic comrades provided him with money to enable him to proceed, though exactly where to was not clear.

How my father got to Trieste I don't know, but I vaguely remember him telling me once that he took an instantaneous liking to this vibrant city, electing to stay a while and then go on *vu di oygn veln mikh trogn* – where his eyes would lead him. As it turned out, the only country prepared to give him a visa was British Palestine, and so he boarded a Greek boat, landing ten days later in Haifa. Once there, he wired his young bride to join him. Which she did, two months later. In due course, I arrived on the scene.

My parents rented a small apartment a short walk from the Tel Aviv beach. The apartment, which I do not remember but which was described to me by my parents, was small, but had all the basic amenities of houses built during the first decades of the century, when Tel Aviv was expanding rapidly. The apartments generally contained one or two bedrooms (ours had one), a dining area, running (cold) water, a primitive kitchen and a bathroom. There were food stores close by, so my mother did not have to walk too far with a small child to get the necessary supplies. The beach was inviting and my mother would spend many hours on it, looking after me and then coming home and preparing dinner for when my father came back from work. I have a photograph of one of those blissful days, with my mother smiling languidly and myself, curled at her feet, laughing into the camera. They had very little money, but she later recalled this period as the happiest time in her life. And no doubt it was. Politically, Palestine was enjoying relative tranquility. My father worked hard, digging ditches, hauling stones in the rising Tel Aviv harbor, distributing Yiddish books, and he earned a bit extra for the odd article he wrote for the Warsaw Bund newspaper, *di naye folkstsaytung*. But my parents were young, the neighbors, many of them the same age, were friendly, I was healthy and apparently good-humored, the sun shone almost every day, and there were no Polish winters (or policemen) to worry about.

My father, who like nearly all Jewish boys of his generation had attended a *kheyder* (religious school), boasted more than a smattering of Hebrew, but my mother had none, and had to take a course designed for non-Hebrew-speaking adults, a forerunner of the later *ulpan* designed to assimilate refugees into Israeli society. They spoke Yiddish to each other, but Hebrew to me, since Yiddish was frowned upon by the leaders of the nascent Jewish state. (Most of them had grown up in that language – Ben Gurion's first job upon arriving in Palestine in 1906 was to edit a Yiddish newspaper for his fellow settlers – but regarded it as part of a distasteful Diaspora legacy to be supplanted by Hebrew, the language of their ancient forebears and of the Jewish future.) My parents had no sympathy for the political ideas of Zionism nor for the zealous efforts to create a new Hebrew culture, but for the time being they concluded, sensibly, that I should be raised in the same language as all other children around us. My mother even learned a few children's songs, which she would sing to me at bedtime. One of them, "The Beautiful Bird" (*tsipor yafa*), I remember to this day, since it remained a favorite of hers long after we had left Palestine and Hebrew behind us.

A brief digression: More than seven million Jews lived in the Russian Empire before the Revolution, and the countries later carved out of it – Poland, Lithuania, Estonia and Latvia. Ninety percent of them, according to the census of 1898, claimed Yiddish as their mother tongue. In the census taken in independent Poland in 1931, 79 percent of all Jews also claimed Yiddish as their mother tongue.

For most Zionists around the turn of the century, Yiddish held few attractions. Many were linguistically assimilated (Herzl himself, the founder of the world Zionist movement, did not know a word of Yiddish), and many of those who knew it scorned Yiddish as a *zhargon*, a debased dialect of German rather than a *bona fide* language. A few Labor Zionist organizations, while insisting that Hebrew be enshrined as the language of the Jewish Homeland, nevertheless acknowledged the importance of Yiddish in the diaspora, and used it in their political and educational work. One of these organizations, the Left Poale Zion, an offshoot of the far larger middle-of-the-road Poale Zion Party, embraced a militant Marxism and a sycophantic attitude towards the Soviet Union, and called for an Arab-Jewish state with Yiddish as one the country's official languages, Arabic the other. (This bizarre amalgam was finally abjured in 1950, when the Left Poale Zion party was merged into the left-wing but more conventional Zionist Mapam.)

The Bund, however, gravitated towards the use of Yiddish in all its activities. The vast majority of workers spoke Yiddish, and the Bund would address them in their language. This, said its leaders, was essential if they were to reach their constituents, and also persuade them of the *khshives* (dignity) of their language and of their Jewish identity in general.

In time this largely pragmatic approach turned into outright championship of Yiddish and the expanding Yiddish secular culture. The Bund set about building Yiddish schools, libraries, summer camps, and other institutions. All these endeavors were subsumed under the theory of *doikayt* (loosely, "here-ness") and "national cultural autonomy", advocated by the Bund in conditions of semi-legality in Tsarist Russia, and also after it metamorphosed into an open political party in independent Poland.

The Bund became the major champion of *Yiddishkayt* in Poland. Many Yiddish writers and poets found in the Bund a source of grateful readers and a support system: the Bund was ready to send them on lecture tours all over the country. A number of them joined the party, while others preferred to be known as "sympathizers," technically unaffiliated but active participants in Bund programs. Many sympathizers lent their support to the Bund at times of the party's greatest trials, voted for the Bund in elections to Jewish and general administrative bodies (such as city councils), and some wrote verse which, set to music (also by Bund sympathizers), was incorporated into the repertoires of choral groups, Yiddish schools, and the Bund's children and youth organizations, SKIF (Socialist Children's Association) and *Tsukunft* (Future).

It is this distinctive world that my parents left in the early 1920s, and to this world they decided to return in late 1929. Why return? To begin with, as I noted earlier, they had come to Palestine not as fervent Zionists, and not (like so many others) because life in Poland was gradually getting grimmer, especially for Jews, so they had no ideological commitment to remain. Their life in Palestine, whatever the lure of the Mediterranean beaches, was not exactly easy, especially for my father. But the most compelling reason was an invitation from the Bund to take over as administrator of a new children's institution established a few years earlier in a wooded village some ten miles from Warsaw: the Medem Sanatorium, named for Vladimir Medem, a revered leader of the Bund. My mother, who held a diploma in nursing, was told that for her, too, a place would be found in the new institution. Anyway, lying on the sand and hauling stones did not represent the sort of life my parents were eager to pursue for years without end – especially if the ultimate reward, a Jewish state, was neither very likely nor very alluring in the first place. The idea of running an institution dedicated both to improving the physical health of impoverished children and to instilling them with socialist and secular Jewish values was clearly a more attractive proposition.

Besides, the atmosphere in Palestine had deteriorated. The nationalism of a people whom thirty years earlier the founders of Zionism had casually dismissed ("a land without people for a people without a land," in one of Zionism's catchiest slogans) was growing, though most Zionist leaders disregarded it. Thus the heads of the Jewish workers' organizations maintained that the Arabs had the Jews to thank for their rising standard of living, and ignored the disparity between it and the far more dramatic rise in the Jewish workers' standard of living. In addition, the Zionist leaders did not win Arab friends when they refused to incorporate Arabs into the Histadrut (Zionist trade union organization), thus in fact forcing the Arabs to accept far lower wages than those paid to Jewish workers.

The tensions between the Yishuv, the Jewish community in Palestine, and the Arabs escalated, finally erupting in the late 1920s in a series of Arab riots which caused the deaths of 133 Jews and 87 Arabs, and many wounded. This may have proved the last straw for my parents; it certainly seemed to validate the Bund's argument that Jews, however many of them settled in Palestine, would be exposed to a greater threat from a fiercely hostile population of 200 million Arabs than from anti-Semitism in Poland. So my parents decided: they – we – would go home.

After arriving in Poland, we first visited my father's relatives in Vilna. Once the proud capital of the Lithuanian-Polish Commonwealth, and still coveted by Lithuania as its ancient capital, Vilna was in those days a poor and provincial city, consisting mainly of wooden houses, with horse-drawn carriages (*droshky*) providing the only means of transportation. We spent much of the time around a big table with a large samovar at its center, sipping tea from glasses, and helping ourselves to large portions of *varenie* (jam, mostly strawberry). I fell in love with this wonderful custom and years later, in Warsaw, I kept imploring my parents to buy a samovar. (They never did.) Vilna felt very much a Russian city, despite the fact that Russians constituted only a minority of its multi-ethnic population: one could hear a lot of Russian on the streets, as well as Polish, Yiddish and Lithuanian. Two years later, on another trip to Vilna, I paid my first visit to a dentist, who operated his drill by stepping on a foot-pedal. All these years later, I shudder at this grim memory, but he thought that I behaved admirably, and told my waiting parents that they obviously had *a tayern bokher* – a dear lad. This pleased both of them, especially my mother. The first stay in Vilna ended after a week or so. We proceeded to Warsaw, or rather to Miedzeszyn, where we moved into a graceful villa abutting the Medem Sanatorium. Whether I should attend nursery school or kindergarten in Miedzeszyn, or whether we should take up residence in Warsaw, was waived for the time being: it was summertime, and there was time to decide.

I shed my first language, Hebrew, shortly after our arrival from Palestine, and switched smoothly to Yiddish. In the process I forgot my Hebrew – not unusual in young children – except for two words that remained firmly imbedded in my vocabulary: *ima* (mother) and *aba* (father). I continued using these words as long as my parents lived, often with diminutive Yiddish endings: *ima-le* and *aba-le*. This oddity was also accepted by our closest relatives and friends, who would inquire, in deference to me, *vos makht di ima*? (how is mother?), or *vu iz der aba*? (where is father?). It never occurred to me, even in my adult years, that there was something unusual about the use of these terms, nor did it seem to occur to my parents. In the kindergarten, the so-called *freblówka* (frebLOOvka, named after Friedrich Froebel, the early 19th-century founder of the kindergarten) and later on, in the Yiddish elementary school, my parents were designated conventionally as *mame* and *tate*.

I spoke Yiddish, of course – but which Yiddish? This seemingly odd, even esoteric question mattered a great deal, because the various dialects of Yiddish had fascinating social implications, in my own case affecting my relations with school friends on the one hand, and with my parents and their friends on the other. In central Poland and in Warsaw the predominant dialect was the "Polish" one, while the northeastern (*litvak*, or Lithuanian) dialect prevailed in Lithuania, Latvia, and Northern Russia. (The "Galician" dialect, somewhat close to the Polish, was spoken in the Ukraine and southern Russia.) The differences consist mostly in the pronunciation of vowels and diphthongs, but also in the use of certain words incomprehensible to the speakers of one dialect or the other. Above all, a social connotation adhered to one and the other. Many of the intelligentsia, educated in Lithuania, regarded the Warsaw dialect as uncouth, spoken by the uneducated classes. This, of course, was a slur: the great novelist Isaac Bashevis Singer, for instance, spoke pure Warsaw Yiddish. *Litvak* Yiddish, however, was what might be called the Oxbridge version, almost identical with "classical" or "literary" Yiddish, as authenticated by the leading Yiddish linguists, most of whom, not surprisingly, hailed from Lithuania and Latvia.

Nonetheless, a slur is a powerful thing, and when I later attended public school in Warsaw, I dared not use the Litvak dialect, lest my school mates (a fairly rough bunch) mock me as a snob. On the other hand, once I stepped over the threshold of our home, I could speak only the Yiddish of my parents and most of their friends. I was altogether fluent in the Warsaw dialect, but my friends knew that I wasn't really one of them, and taunted me repeatedly for my "Litvak airs." My situation vis-à-vis my classmates resembled my position in the sanatorium as the deputy director's son: on the one hand I wanted to belong to the majority, on the other I felt somewhat superior to it. The result was pain, resentment, envy, and a sense of persecution. When I walked home, a small band of juveniles always followed me, hollering derisive remarks (*litvak khazer* – Litvak pig – was one of the favorites). Nevertheless I loved the school with a passion and would often regale my parents with stories of my scholastic achievements and various school events.

Then there was the matter of Polish, the state language, which all children were expected to know, and which was also used in the courses of Polish literature and Polish history in the Yiddish secular schools, whereall other subjects, from geography to arithmetic to biology, were taught in Yiddish. My knowledge of Polish was flawed, since most of my friends spoke Yiddish and only a few of them came from assimilated homes where Polish predominated; furthermore, I had no gentile friends at all. This did not stop me from being a rather fervent Polish patriot: lack of contact with gentiles was due to the prevailing anti-Semitism, and that, my Bundist mentors taught me, was but a passing phase that would have no place in the future socialist society.

2

Growing up a Socialist

*The sanatorium as utopia. mir kumen on. How I became class
conscious. Socialism vs. anti-Semitism. The Yiddish school
and other organizations. The Bund victorious.*

The Medem Sanatorium was, despite its title, far more than a health institution providing daily medical care, good food, clean air and plenty of rest to poor children suffering from respiratory and other ailments. It was at the same time the embodiment of a socialist dream - the proudest creation of the Bund, a veritable children's republic, a model of the future socialist state. Its principles were not conceived as mere declarations of noble intent. They were designed to be incorporated in the very structure and *modus operandi* of the institution, in the children's daily lives and their relations with one another. Cultivating a sense of freedom, of mutual regard, and of self-reliance was one part of the sanatorium's élan; the other, in line with the national ideology of the Bund, was a respect for one's people and love of the Yiddish language and culture.

Accordingly, many activities were performed by the children themselves. The children looked after the sanatorium's chickens and incubators at the Biological Station; they checked on personal cleanliness; they made the beds and folded the blankets every morning, and so on. The *sanatoristn* also participated in regular assemblies and elected a "children's council" (*kinderrat*) responsible for coordinating the various activities and adjudicating cases of minor disciplinary infractions. The reigning language, of course, was Yiddish, and children unable to speak it freely quickly became proficient in it. All supervisors were addressed as "teacher" (*lerer* for men, *lererin* for women), followed by their last names. (I had a crush on *lererin* Zakheym, a graceful woman in her late twenties, with short hair and a winsome smile.)

In 1935 a leading Polish film director, Alexander Ford, made a film about the sanatorium called *mir kumen on* (Here we come). The film's title came from the sanatorium's most popular song, written by the music teacher Yankev Trupiansky, a tall swarthy man in his thirties, with a prominent nose and a shock of pitch-black hair: *a yontev makht oyf ale merk/un fayern tsindt on oyf berg/mir kumen, shturem on a tsam/fun land tsu land, fun yam tsu yam!* Let fairs start up in market-squares/And bonfires blaze on hills/For here we come: a storm out of bounds/From land to land, from sea to sea! The film (in which I appear for a breathless moment) is half-documentary, half-scripted, and ends with a group of youngsters (among them Marek Edelman, later one of the leaders of the Warsaw Ghetto Uprising), arms linked, striding forward beneath a cloudless sky and lustily singing *mir kumen on*.

The Polish authorities banned the film, on the grounds that it was "anti Polish" and "pro-communist," specious nonsense characteristic of the xenophobic mentality of the politicians who ruled Poland at that time. Abroad, the film received great acclaim and even won the first prize at a festival of documentary films in France. In 1936, my father took *mir kumen* on on a fund-raising trip to France, where he was introduced by fellow-socialists to French cuisine, an experience he later recounted with awe. ("Can you believe it?" I remember him saying to my mother, "at the restaurant my friends asked the waiter to bring them a slab of raw meat which they inspected carefully and only then sent it back to the kitchen to be cooked. Now, there is civilization for you!") This and meeting Leon Blum were the two highlights of his visit. (A year later he took the film to London: the high point of that visit was a meeting with one of the Labor Party's luminaries, Herbert Morrison).

I have a copy of the film at home, and from time to time I look at it, always falling under its spell. It has some painfully naïve scenes that make me squirm. But most of it is remarkably honest, devoid of sentimentality, the children charming and believable, the humor gentle, the staff - teachers, nurses, gardeners - exactly as I remember them, dedicated and coolly matter-of-fact. One of the sanatorium's great finds was a young boy, Arele Hochberg, already an accomplished violinist at age nine, who performs the first movement of a violin concerto by Vivaldi before an audience of transfixed *sanatoristn*, their legs under the table swinging to the sound of the music. (Hochberg went to France in 1939 to continue his studies, there to perish in 1942.)

In another touching scene, symbolic of the Bund's determination to display its loyalty to Polish culture, a winsome 10-year-old girl performs two songs, the first in Yiddish and the second in Polish. The children are shown delightedly applauding both the one and the other. The film also showed a scene, based on a real incident, of a number of Polish children of striking miners, their faces taut and astonished, being brought to the sanatorium and showered - bilingually - with love and affection, in a poignant expression of socialist class solidarity. (Most Polish educators hailed the scene; the authorities detested it.)

During my father's second trip with the film, which lasted several weeks, I joined the SKIF (*sotsialistisher kinder farband*, socialist children's association), the children's branch of the Bund. Proud of my new credentials, I remember greeting my father at the train station as he was stepping onto the platform with the words "Aba, I am now class conscious." My father smiled gently and later greatly enjoyed telling his friends of the charming surprise that awaited him upon his return from abroad. A week or so thereafter I sprung another surprise: the SKIF group I joined, along with a few other new children, would be named after Karl Marx - at my suggestion. A generous man, my father refrained from commenting on this novel idea.

As a *skifist*, I attended bi-weekly meetings, though I don't remember what transpired at them. I wrote some doggerel called "May Day," which the editor of the children's page of the Bundist daily, *folkstsaytung*, (inexplicably) thought fit to publish. I also joined the Bund youth athletic club *morgnshtern* (Morning Star), and every Monday and Thursday afternoon, together with my friends, would join in strenuous physical exercises or a game of soccer. One Sunday morning we marched, eight abreast, in our blue shirts and red ties (outfits of the same color as, but never to be confused with, those worn by our adversaries on Red Square) to the Warsaw Circus, where hundreds of *skifistn* and members of the Bund's Youth Organization *tsukunft* (Future) displayed their athletic skills before a cheering crowd. Occasionally we would burst into song, favoring such rousing numbers as "We the Young Guard of the Proletariat:" *dem morgnroyt antkegn/vi nor di zun dershaynt/farnemen mir di vegn/ zol tsitern der faynt*; At dawn's early light/We flood all the roads/Let the foe tremble with fear!

Like other European youth organizations, the SKIF had an affinity for the Great Outdoors. I longed to join one of its summer camps, but was considered too young. I did, however, somehow manage to get into a winter camp held one bitterly cold week in late 1938. The participants, about thirty young boys and girls, were housed in a simple villa somewhere in the countryside. I remember getting up every morning at five-thirty to the piercing sound of a bugle, making my bed, hurriedly dressing and then running through the snow to a nearby forest. The sun was barely out, the air a curtain of ice; we would then dash back to the villa and burn our mouths on cups of scalding cocoa.

Our leader was a young man by the name of Emanuel Pat, who later became a well-known physician in the Bronx. Our daily program consisted of gymnastics, learning new songs and the odd lecture delivered by Pat or other speakers from the Bund sent down from Warsaw for that purpose. The winter camp lasted ten days and, despite the daily morning maledictions hurled at us by young Polish bullies, we returned invigorated, our ideological batteries recharged.

As a pupil of a secular Yiddish school and a *skifist*, I was also offered a minor role in a play about the French Revolution, probably stitched together by some of our teachers and acted by the pupils of the Yiddish schools. The play was performed on the stage of the Nowości Theater in Warsaw, a Jewish-owned establishment where many Yiddish plays were produced. Of that rousing drama I recall only running around in torn trousers, one of the many sans-culottes, and singing "O, ça ira, ça ira, ça ira, les aristocrats à la lanterne!" We confined our French to that song: otherwise the play was entirely in Yiddish.

Another play produced at the same theater was a Yiddish translation of a whimsical poem by the Soviet children's writer S. Marshak, called "Mister Tvister." One of the sanatorium's beloved teachers, Batke Gilinsky, wrote the Yiddish text, and the indomitable Yankev Trupiansky composed the music. (Both Gilinsky and Trupiansky perished in the Holocaust.) The story line posed something of a quandary for the Bundist producers, since it was all about a pompous American plutocrat (*Mister Tvister, gevezener* [former] *minister, Mister Tvister milyoner...*) who comes to the Soviet Union, where he finds himself overwhelmed by its sprit of equality, optimism and solicitude for all its citizens.

Neither our ideological mentors (nor the country's censors) could be expected to abide this message, so the venue was changed: Mister Tvister kept his identity, but the action all took place on a boat, a kind of floating utopia whose denizens found their American passenger too absurd for words... I played the role of an absent-minded professor, and still have a photograph of myself in that role, a tribute to the skill of our make-up artist. (In 1999 I happened to see a performance of "Mister Tvister" in Moscow: it struck me as decidedly inferior to our Warsaw Yiddish version.)

Another important event in my socialist childhood were the annual May Day demonstrations, to which I always looked forward with avid excitement. The Bund and the Left Poale Zion (left-wing Labor Zionists) – the only Jewish political grouping with which the Bund would collaborate – jointly sponsored some of the demonstrations; others included the PPS (Polish Socialist Party). The Communists, who did not command a big following and were in fact illegal, could not march under their own banners; instead, many would march under the banners of the trade unions they dominated.

It was exhilarating to see the flushed faces of the marching men and women, the massed red flags, the banners proclaiming LONG LIVE THE FRIENDSHIP OF ALL WORKERS and DOWN WITH FASCISM (in Yiddish and Polish), the ranks flanked by cane-swinging members of the Bund's defense militia. The Zionist socialist groups, such as the Hashomer Hatzair, were also accompanied by their own defense units, as was the PPS. The police were everywhere but did not interfere, and almost all the demonstrations passed without incident.

Usually my mother took me to watch the parade. Her maternal feelings seemed to outweigh her party loyalty – she preferred observing, with me at her side, to striding with her fellow-Bundists - but I was always on the lookout for my father marching by. Once, in front of the huge Polish National Theater, still standing in Warsaw today, I detached myself from my mother, and, breaking through the ranks of the militia, joined the marchers. A militiaman turned me around, pushed me towards the spectators and sternly admonished me not to do it again.

Of all the institutions that contributed to my socialist-cum-Jewish upbringing, the most important by far was the daily secular school, maintained by the *tsisho*, Central Yiddish School Organization, an alliance primarily of the Bund and the small Left Poale Zion but also embracing representatives of several other Yiddish secular groups. The schools taught all their subjects in Yiddish except Polish, Polish literature and history of Poland. Some did not include Hebrew in their curricula, others did. Vilna schools, for instance, tended to include Hebrew more often than schools in central Poland and Galicia (Ukraine). Though generally considered pedagogically superior to the other Jewish schools, the *tsisho* schools attracted a relatively small percentage of Jewish children in Poland. There was close competition from the Tarbut ("culture" in Hebrew) schools, where the language of instruction was Hebrew (even though by far more Jews spoke Yiddish than Hebrew), from orthodox religious schools, and also from special schools for Jewish children maintained by the state (the so-called *szabasówki*, which were closed on Saturdays). For some religious parents the determinedly secular/socialist character of the Yiddish schools made them unacceptable. Still, the Yiddish schools, plus the SKIF, plus the Medem Sanatorium, played a disproportionately prominent part in Jewish education in Poland.[1]

I attended two schools. The first, named after Joseph Khmurner, one of the leaders of the Bund's "left faction" (the faction, though out of tune with the majority of Bund members, nevertheless had full freedom to disseminate its views), was located on Krochmalna Street, made internationally famous by the works of the Yiddish writer and Nobel Prize winner Isaac Bashevis Singer, who grew up there. Krochmalna Street was right smack in the center of Jewish poverty: noisy, crowded, dirty and host to itinerant groups of Jewish singers, clowns, magicians and the like, who would perform in the courtyards of the buildings. These courtyards connected one to another, thus affording escape routes for groups of petty thieves "working" in that area.

The school, consisting of grades two to seven, held classes on the third floor of a shabby building, Krochmalna 36, in several classrooms and one large room used for gymnastics and physical exercise (taught by the ubiquitous Trupiansky, obviously a man of parts). Already in grade Three I gained the reputation of a stormy petrel (a *łobuz* in Polish, or *shtifer*, in Yiddish), given to organizing earsplitting activities intended to drive the teachers to distraction – and often successful. More than once I would gather together a bunch of boys my age, and lead them in a procession through the school, singing at the top of our lungs a Polish song we considered the acme of revolutionary fervor: *Nasze kiszki marsza grają/Żądamy chleba!/A jak chleba nie chcą dać/Szturmem go brać!* (Our insides play a march/We demand bread!/And if we receive no bread/We'll take it by storm!).

In 1936, my parents could afford to move out of their sublet rooms into their own apartment, and we moved to one that, to my delight, included a room of my own. Our courtyard led to a second yard that in winter metamorphosed into a skating rink, with Strauss waltzes playing on a tinny Victrola and young men and women careening around, bumping into one another. Partly as a result of our move, my parents transferred me to another Yiddish school, in a rough neighborhood. Apparently they were also swayed by the gentle encouragement of the Khmurner principal: my behavior had so distressed the math teacher, a venerable man by the name of Pollak, that he'd told her either he or I must leave the premises. (Needless to say, I was rather proud of myself when I learned about it, though I do not know to this day whether there was any truth to it.)

One of my new teachers, a bony young man called Grinberg, was infatuated with the works of the great Yiddish writer I.L. Peretz. Grinberg once organized a "trial" of one of Peretz's most affecting heroes, the self-effacing Bontshe Schweig (Bontshe the Silent), who when offered the reward of his choice in the afterlife, requested merely a roll and butter. (The custom of staging "literary trials," incidentally, was widespread in all the *tsisho* schools.) Did Bontshe deserve to go to Heaven for his modesty and diffidence, or did his behavior reflect moral defeatism? The pupils argued fiercely (the teachers did not interfere) and in the end not surprisingly condemned Bontshe for cravenness: he should, the pupils decided, have stood up for his rights and not let the world crush him into morbid passivity.

Growing up as a *skifist* also meant participating in some of the political battles waged by the parent party. In November 1938 groups of *skifistn*, myself included, marched through the streets of Warsaw, handing out flyers and yelling in unison: *eyns, tsvey, dray, fir: shtimt far liste numer fir!* (one, two, three, four: cast your vote for number four, list number four being that of the Bund's candidates.) Once my group saw approaching a similar group of youngsters urging the election of the Zionist list: we turned right around, and headed off in the opposite direction, not wishing to become involved in any altercations. That year – though not necessarily due to our efforts - the Bund won significant victories to the elections of city councils in Warsaw, Lodz, and other cities, thus becoming the strongest Jewish political party at that time. It was a sign of the times: the country was becoming radicalized. The victory was particularly prominent in Warsaw, where the Bund won nearly all of the votes cast for Jewish parties, leaving the Zionists and Agudas Israel (orthodox) far behind. Among the new city council members was my father, whose life, accordingly, became a never-ending trek from home to sanatorium to council meetings, back home late at night, and early in the morning again to the sanatorium. Consequently, I saw less and less of him.

To grow up as a secular socialist also meant reading works both of Yiddish authors and European authors in translation: Dickens, Kipling, Selma Lagerlof, Knut Hamsun, Jack London and others. *The Call of the Wild* was the favorite of a generation of Jewish schoolchildren, as was the more horrific *The Sea Wolf*. Kastner's wonderful fantasy *Emil and the Detectives* was a big hit, and a theatrical version was often performed in children's theaters. A friend of mine had all the works of Jules Verne in Yiddish prominently displayed on his bookshelf. I borrowed them, one by one. I loved them all, but my favorite, not surprisingly, was *Michael Strogoff*: Tsarist Russia was more part of my universe than the moon, the jungles of Borneo, or the depths of the Pacific Ocean.

I also devoured books by Polish authors: Henryk Sienkiewicz, Bolesław Prus, Stefan Żeromski. Good Yiddishists we were, to be sure, but also loyal to Poland, and Polish fiction of the late 19th and early 20th centuries bolstered our patriotism. I took it for granted that my friends and I, equally firm in both our Jewishness and our allegiance to Poland, took pride in Poland's achievements (number five in coal production!). We gloried in the exploits of the 18th century revolutionary Tadeusz Kosciuszko and in the fact that Marie Curie Skłodowska was a Pole.

Oddly enough I never seemed to crave the friendship of Polish children, and young gentiles seemed hardly to notice us except to shout abuse that I did not always fully comprehend. Once when my parents and I were returning from a visit somewhere, I heard a group of boys shouting derisively "*Starozakonni, starozakonni!*" and had to ask my father what that meant. "Followers of the Old Testament," he explained, but I was still baffled. We were Jews, of course, but not followers of the Old Testament, whatever that was; surely they meant those Hassidic boys one saw on certain streets, with their side curls and long black coats? They, too, were Jews, of course - but not my Jews...

Poland in the late 1930s was awash with anti-Semitic passions. Jewish stores were attacked, and their owners beaten up; Jewish students were forced to occupy special "ghetto benches" in the universities and were preyed upon by razor-wielding bands of hoodlums. The government advocated policies designed to deprive the Jews of any rights whatsoever, its intent to force the Jews to emigrate, thus making the country *Judenrein*. So how, in such conditions, did we manage to combine our assertive Jewishness with Polish patriotism? Even more curiously, how did many of us grow up in so paradoxical a climate without suffering irreparable emotional damage? I believe the explanation lies in one of the central ingredients of my upbringing: "internationalism," which is to say, socialism. Not Soviet-style "socialism," a betrayal - I was taught - of true socialist beliefs, but a doctrine rooted in equality, individual freedom and democracy. Our ideology combined the belief that Jews had the right to remain in Poland with the conviction that we also had the right to build our lives and institutions in our own language, Yiddish. We were certain that eventually our ideals would prevail. The sense of security that I derived from these beliefs and that certitude gave me the strength to reject the temptations of other ideologies swirling around at that time. It was an odd mélange, but it worked.

The events described in this and the previous chapter do not comprise one of those "vanishing" worlds to which my book is dedicated. They constitute, emphatically and indisputably, a world vanished in its entirety, destroyed, extirpated, leaving no trace of anything but memories. Nothing whatever remains of the Medem Sanatorium, as I had occasion to find out several years ago. A good Polish friend of mine, Wiktor Kulerski, once published a description of the excruciating 1942 deportation of Jewish men, women and children from the areas surrounding Warsaw. Among them were also the children of the sanatorium, who were loaded onto trains and dispatched, with the teachers and nurses, to the gas ovens in Treblinka. In the 1970s Kulerski visited the grounds of the sanatorium and took some photographs, and in 1982 he, Marek Edelman and I drove out to see whether anything remained of the old structures. Nothing did. Only a small memorial stone with a brief inscription stood nearby. It read: "Here, upon these grounds, the Home Army Maintained a Home for Polish Children, 1942-45." The Home was obviously organized after the sanatorium was liquidated. But the stone carried not a word about what existed there before. We stood there, in silence, Kulerski, Edelman, and I, and then turned and left, determined never to return again.

3

September 1939: from Warsaw to Vilna

War tremors. Gymnazjum and war. Farewell, Warsaw. mishpokhedikayt. oyf gots barot. From Luniniec to Lunin. The Red Army takes over. Vilna in our dreams.

In the last few weeks of August 1939, the mood on the streets of Warsaw grew tense. People were scurrying back and forth buying up *prowianty* (food staples) and leisurely encounters, especially on the *deptak* - the area where young men would meet their dates for an evening stroll - were becoming rare. The weather was mild, as late summer and early autumn in central Poland can be, the ordinary life of a city interrupted by the occasional wails of sirens, the sight of people taping their windows crosswise to prevent splintering should bombs start falling (but would they? but would they? it all seemed weird and unreal), long queues forming in front of banks from which silent couples exited, clutching their transaction slips as they went home, there to take stock of their accumulated savings and make crucial decisions: to stash them away, to take part with them if they left Warsaw (but how?), possibly to entrust them to old friends or trustworthy servants not contemplating fleeing the city. (Needless to say, this concerned only the relatively affluent - the bulk of Varsovians carried on, equally anxious but with even fewer options.)

The days were getting shorter, and so were people's tempers. Some thought the panic unfounded: the war is not yet upon us, they said, and it may well be averted. The Germans are adroit in spreading hysteria, while themselves no doubt trembling in their boots. Anyway, who knows? The French and the English may finally cast the die for immediate mobilization, and unnerve the Germans with a massive threat to the Siegfried Line, and with hundreds of Spitfires ready to rain destruction on the German forces. (The role of the grand Polish cavalry did not figure prominently even in these wishful scenarios.)

The German-Soviet Non-Aggression Pact, signed in Moscow on August 23, shattered the city's uneasy tranquility like a thunderbolt. Those who had derided the spreading panic now began to yield to it themselves. Twelve years old, I was not in Warsaw myself during those last few weeks of the summer, only occasionally accompanying my mother on a shopping expedition to the capital. We remained at the Medem Sanatorium, about 10 miles outside of Warsaw, although the Sanatorium directors decided to begin sending the children home in the middle of August. In those tense weeks, to expect the worst was merely to be sensible.

As August drew to an end, only a small skeleton staff stayed on: a few nurses, teachers, and kitchen personnel. I remember helping to dig trenches in the orchard and covering them with twigs, in case of air raids. My father was in charge of closing down the premises and storing away the valuables, such as radio crystals, the public address equipment and so on. (As we learned later, the much-beloved Belorussian watchman, Maxim Maximenko, soon exhumed all the effects, placing some in his cottage and selling the rest to the local peasants. When the Germans came, he offered his services to them.)

On the morning of September 1, my father and I took the local *elektrowka* (electric train) from Miedzeszyn to Warsaw, and thence to Żoliborz, a northern suburb of Warsaw, where I was to take my entrance exam to the local *gymnazjum*. My parents decided on that particular school because, like most of Żoliborz, it was known for its progressive ambience. In fact the school board was dominated by the PPS (Polish Socialist Party), and did not discriminate against Jewish students. For a Jewish child, then, particularly one from a Bundist environment, this was obviously a most desirable choice. I remember my father taking me to the exam hall, and then retiring, after an encouraging smile and handshake.

I have no recollection of the questions I was asked to answer nor the topics for short essays, though I am sure that any relating to mathematics made me break out in a cold sweat. I do remember that the exam room was very quiet, the silence broken only by the lone examiner pacing between rows of heads bent over desks covered with blue notebooks and white question sheets. Not a sound reached us from the outside.

After three hours, the examiner collected all the notebooks and told us we were free to go. As I made my way to the hallway I saw my father, smiling, I thought, rather disconsolately. I still remember his greeting: "Son, we are at war." After a while, he asked me how the exam went, but I was too stunned to answer. We took a streetcar to the train station. Years later I read in some memoirs that the whole Polish air force was annihilated on the ground the first day of the war, and that not a single Polish plane succeeded in engaging the enemy aircraft. But that is not the way I remember it. As we arrived at the train station, I could see clearly above us planes firing at each other, and one of them catapulting to the ground, a long sash of white smoke trailing behind it. Two hours later, when the elektrowka deposited us in Miedzeszyn, there were no *bryczkas* (horse-drawn carriages) to be had, and so we walked through the woods and then through a wide meadow leading to the sanatorium, neither of us saying a word. In the distance, we could see thin streaks of smoke jutting into the sky.

The next few days were eerie. More personnel departed, especially those who came from places far from Warsaw. My parents and friends sat hunched around the radio for hours, listening to the news. It was not cheerful. France and England declared war on Germany, but in the meantime the Polish forces were falling back, the Germans moving ahead at a rapid clip, and it looked as if they would soon be in the environs of Warsaw.

On September 5, the Polish government declared Warsaw an "open city," and urged all able-bodied men to head east, there to be drafted into new fighting units. In response, my parents and five members of the staff decided to leave the sanatorium. The only transport was by horse and cart, the driver to be given money to take us as far east as he was willing to go. There was no time to go to Warsaw to fetch additional belongings. Anyway, there would be no room for them on the *furmanka* (coach). By that time, I had nearly forgotten the *gymnazjum* in Żoliborz.

On the morning of our departure, I took a quick stroll through the sanatorium grounds, stopping at the sights I treasured most: the orchard, the *natur vinkl* ("nature corner"), the now-emptied *hiner shtaygn* (chicken coops), the care of which was one of the children's favorite activities, and the *alte gebayde* (old building), one of the two main structures in the sanatorium, where I had slept for the past ten nights, listening every night to dogs howling in the distance, alone in a room that usually housed many children.

The hard boards of the *furmanka* were softened with large pillows, amidst which seven of us - six adults and I - placed ourselves, with the coachman in front. A short, wiry man, he waited quietly until we loaded our belongings on the cart, then cracked his whip, and we were off. I felt my chest constricting with pain as I took the last glance at the sanatorium, while at the same time a strange sense of excitement came over me: what, I wondered, was in store for us next?

The road was crammed with horse-driven vehicles of all descriptions, automobiles, motorcycles, lorries big and small and also, increasingly, by pedestrians pushing carts or carrying bags on their backs. One of our group, until recently a member of the sanatorium's teaching staff, told me that these people were heading east or south to put as much distance as possible between themselves and the advancing German troops, with some hoping to cross the border into Romania. Some of the men on foot or in vehicles were counting on getting drafted into the army somewhere along the way, though in fact that rarely occurred. "And what about us?" I asked. My father shrugged his shoulders.

Save for the itinerant humanity, there was little on the road to engage my attention. Most of the passengers on the *furmanka* were quiet, preoccupied and lost in thought. I don't remember what we did about food, but I am sure we carried some sandwiches and perhaps some cold milk, enough for what little appetites we had.

In the early evening, around six, we stopped in a small village: this was as far as the *furman* (coachman) would take us. Luckily there was already a committee of local Bundists on hand, formed precisely for such emergencies: everybody in the village expected groups of comrades from Warsaw. It was a splendid instance of Bundist *mishpokhedikayt* ("familiness"), an intense sense of loyalty felt by Bundists to each other and to the movement. We were greeted like old friends, though none of us knew the local comrades personally, and taken to several homes where we washed, ate, and went to sleep. I recall being directed to a large bed where another three or four children were spending the night: a "first" for me, a child of middle class parents, used to sleeping in my own bed and even, the last few years, in my own room.

The following morning a new *furman* and cart were found, and the trek resumed. Only a few things stand out in my memory from the next two days. One is the increasing number of abandoned cars on the highway: gas was nowhere to be gotten. Another is going through the fairly large town of Siedlce, which had just been bombed. One side of the main street was in flames, the other was untouched. All the houses were small, two or at most three stories high. It was an eerie scene: one side of the long street extending from one end of the town to the other consumed by flame and smoke, the other pristine, untouched. The German bombers had swooped over the town only a short while before.

At one point, a number of people, clearly agitated, stopped our cart, and asked us to take a wounded woman to the local hospital. A middle-aged peasant, she was lying on a huge pillow soaked in blood. My mother, a professional nurse, attended to her. My father and I jumped off the cart, and continued to follow on foot. We reached the hospital in a few minutes, a small, wooden one-storied building besieged by lorries, carts and private automobiles discharging their wounded passengers, one of them, I noted in mute horror, with a nearly severed arm dangling bloodily from his side.

The vehicles hurried on, and so did we, after depositing the wounded woman. I walked next to my father, and saw his eyes filling with tears: a shocking sight to a teen-aged boy accustomed to regard his father as a pillar of strength. To this day, the memory of my father with tears in his eyes still sends a shiver down my spine.

Outside Siedlce a German plane appeared from the distance, and we threw ourselves into an adjacent potato field, face down, as we had been instructed to do in such emergencies. I heard the bullets whistling over my head and at one point, turning on my side, saw a soldier aiming his rifle at the airplane. Where did he come from? And what did he mean to accomplish by this pitiable act? It was a bizarre sight.

Two days later, after another stay among solicitous fellow Bundists - all, as in the first *shtetl*, strangers - we arrived in Brest Litovsk, a fortified town where the Bolsheviks, in 1918, signed their humiliating peace treaty with the Germans. Again we were met by the local Bund committee, and directed to a small house built around a courtyard. Again, the owners and children greeted us as if we were close family members returning after a long absence.

After a sumptuous meal, we heard a barrage of sirens, and a few moments later German bombers came over the city. Everybody ran outside into the courtyard, fearfully looking up into the sky: the airplanes were flying only a hundred meters above our heads - or so it seemed. We could see the pilots, and we heard the explosions, some dreadfully close to us. Nearly everyone, that is: my father, in a display of socialist insouciance, refused to budge. He was about to shave and nothing, not even my mother's desperate pleas, was going to bring him outside.

The planes departed after an hour. I don't remember going into the street to survey the damage: perhaps I was afraid of what I would see? I was shaken by the bombing, or perhaps by the accumulated impact of the last several days. My mother stroked my hair, trying to reassure me. My father looked fit and relaxed; I don't know why. But I wanted to escape – into sleep, at least. Luckily, I had a bed to myself that night.

The following morning, we learned that we could continue our trip eastward by train, at least all the way to Pinsk, some 150 kilometers away, center of the Pripet marshes, capital of the province of Polesie. We scanned the skies anxiously through our train windows, but there were no German planes to be seen. Three hours later, we arrived. Pinsk, I knew, was one of Poland's poorest towns. I recall half-empty streets, women in black shawls scurrying alongside the buildings, garbage on the streets, not a store in sight. A few weeks later, Pinsk was to become part of the Ukrainian Socialist Republic, looking confidently forward (as the inhabitants would be told) to a shining future.

This I recall as the low point of our journey: we did not know anyone in Pinsk, no Bundist committee greeted us, and in fact we did not even know in which direction to head, or by what means of locomotion. Finally someone suggested that we set off by foot to Luniniec, a railway center some ten kilometers northeast of Pinsk. That seemed reasonable, and so a few hours later, equipped with rucksacks (where they came from I do not know) we found ourselves in the woods, on a dirt road leading to Luniniec. We were now, as the Yiddish saying has it, *oyf gots barot* - at God's mercy. We proceeded on foot, stopping for the night at some *khata* (hut) where, for a bundle of zlotys, the peasant owner provided us with a loaf of bread, a jug of fresh if tepid milk, just out of the cows' udders, and a place to sleep.

After two days, we arrived, tired and disheveled, at the train center of Luniniec. Here, to our delight, we met two Bundists, a young man named Avreml (Abraham) Zheleznikov, and his charge, the elderly Vladimir Kosovsky, one of founders of the Bund and to me a legendary figure. Zheleznikov was supposed to be guiding Kosovsky to some safe haven, though no one knew whether, let alone where, it existed. We exchanged some excited gossip, asked about friends and comrades and their whereabouts, warmly embraced the two men, and resumed out trek. (Kosovsky, incidentally, eventually came to the United States, and Zheleznikov landed in Melbourne, Australia.)

In Luniniec, where a throng of railroad cars jostled against one another, we discovered that there was only one train to be boarded: where it would go was anyone's guess. And so, utterly exhausted, we piled into an empty open freight car, and waited. Our actions were characteristic of those chaotic days, when no one knew what would happen the next day, and no one even inquired where the train would take us. We found several tattered blankets, covered ourselves as best we could, and went to sleep.

At some point the train started moving, stopping in the early morning when we were informed that the journey, at least for this particular train, was over. We staggered out onto the platform, and found ourselves in a small Ukrainian town called Lunin. Two members of our group were delighted, since this was their hometown and no doubt their parents and relatives were going to be happy to find them alive and well; the rest were relieved to be somewhere known. But as we walked through the tree-lined streets, we felt a peculiar tautness among the townspeople, as if they were trying to avoid or not to look at each other. Soon enough we learned why: we had arrived in Lunin on September 17, the day the Soviet armies entered Eastern Poland to "liberate" their Belorussian and Ukrainian brothers from fascist oppression. The shock, to everyone and particularly to our small group of Bundists, was enormous. Who from now on could be relied upon as a friend, and who might prove to be an enemy? No one knew, of course, of the secret protocol signed by Molotov and Ribbentrop on August 23 specifying the incorporation of most of eastern Poland into the Soviet Union, but the Soviet occupation left little to the imagination.

We spent the next few days in Lunin, my parents hoping soon to leave for Vilna, where part of my father's family resided. Most of the townsfolk went about their business, but here and there one could see local residents with red armbands, part of the newly formed "Red Guard" maintaining order together with the police, and erecting a large welcoming arch, bedecked with red flowers and pictures of Marx, Lenin and Stalin. This was placed over the main street, in expectation of the Soviet army that - rumor said – would soon pass through Lunin.

In the event, the conquering Soviet army consisted of a few officers and enlisted men, who arrived two days later to take over the town – a great disappointment to the local comrades, who had been looking forward to welcoming the "liberators" with bread and salt. We stayed in Lunin four days in the apartment of a local Bundist family. For my father, spending most of the time at our hosts' apartment was a blessing. He did not cherish the prospect of being recognized as a Bundist and thus as "an enemy of the people", all too likely to be detained and delivered into the hands of the Soviet secret police... I cannot remember much about this small, pleasant but otherwise unremarkable little town, except that I was aware of the excitement among the red-armbanded civilians whose number seemed to increase with each day, as did the number of positions they took over from the steadily thinning ranks of the Polish police and officialdom.

We were waiting, impatiently, for news from Vilna, which Soviet troops entered on September 18. Our relatives, we learned, were alive and well. But when would train traffic be resumed?

On the fourth day, it turned out that the tracks to Vilna were clear, and that a train was scheduled to depart the following morning. We were there in plenty of time. At the station, my throat was parched, and my father suggested that I walk up to a Red Army soldier guarding the station, and ask (my father taught me the correct words in Russian) whether he could spare me a drink from his canteen. This was a shock: surely my father would not have been inclined to suggest that I approach a Polish soldier for drink of water! But much as he detested the Communists, he felt that a Russian was apt to be a *khoroshyi paren* (a good lad) and would oblige me. Which indeed he did. I was impressed, and it came to me, sacrilegiously, that perhaps the Bundist hostility to the Communists, which I imbibed at home and in the Bund's children organizations to which I belonged, might not be fully justified. A few weeks later, in Vilna, I was cured of this idea.

4

Vilna 1939-1941

*A world turned topsy-turvy. The charms of Vilna.
Long live khaver Stalin! A curious birthday. My father goes into
hiding. On the move again.*

On the morning of September 23, 1939, my parents and I boarded the train that was to take us to Vilna. A few days earlier, we had welcomed - *façon de parler* - the victorious Red Army come to liberate its Slavic brethren from the oppressive yoke of the Polish *pany* ("sirs"- that is, noblemen) and their "fascist" government in Warsaw. Many years later I would read the accounts by nationalist Polish historians of how the Jewish population in *shtetlekh* such as Lunin cheered the Red Army troops and then flocked to the Soviet security forces to help them apprehend Polish "counterrevolutionaries" (a.k.a Polish "patriots") to be transported under inhuman conditions to Kazakhstan and the Soviet Far East. Barely 13 years old at that time, I was hardly in a position to check the validity of these claims, though I remember vividly the strenuous efforts made by my parents and other Jews to avoid falling into the hands of the Soviet police.

Needless to say, to the Jews even the Soviet police were vastly preferable to the Gestapo that was so busily cleansing of the local "Jewish-Bolshevik scum" the newly captured towns only a few kilometers away. Both sides were implementing the grand 20th century design to divest themselves - and the world - of "undesirable elements," but Jews constituted the intended target for one, and only what we would now call "collateral damage" for the other. We found out later that about one third of the men, women and children seized and deported by the Soviet troops were Jewish. Yet however brutal their fate, most of them escaped with their lives; in fact, about 300,000 Polish Jews survived as a result of finding themselves, in 1939-40, on the Soviet side of the new border. Of the Polish Jews under German occupation, three percent survived.

After three weeks on the road, Vilna seemed idyllic. All the constituents of its heterogeneous population - Russian, Poles, Belorussians, Lithuanians, Jews - could rightly claim it as their own. The seat of the Duchy of Lithuania in the Middle Ages and between 1569-1795 the capital of the Polish-Lithuanian Commonwealth, Vilna then fell into Russian hands and in 1920 was annexed by independent Poland. Its 60,000-strong Jewish community was the seat of Jewish learning, steeped in Yiddish but also host to the Haskala (Enlightenment) and the Hebrew national movements, with newspapers and schools in both languages. The birthplace of the Bund, Vilna had also been at one time or another the headquarters of other Jewish political parties all along the political spectrum. There was something for everyone in Vilna.

For myself and my parents, Vilna was (until something better came along...) precisely where we hoped to end up. It was there that a good number of my father's relatives resided: his mother, sister, brother-in-law, and nine-year-old niece. The near-by shtetl Swieciany was also home to several relatives, who had hosted me a few years earlier for a glorious Passover *seder*. Vilna was the first town we had stopped in during our return from Palestine to Poland in 1930, and we had visited a few times after we moved to Warsaw. For me it was the apotheosis of family life, an atmosphere I sorely missed in our small Warsaw residence, what with my father often staying at the sanatorium till late at night or detained at some meeting at the Warsaw City Council, leaving me and my mother to enjoy each other's lonely company. So there was much to look forward to.

In the event, reality did not disappoint me. We were greeted gleefully at the train station by the whole Pomerantz family, and proceeded right away into their fairly capacious apartment on the first floor of Zawalna Street, one of Vilna's main thoroughfares and the location, a few blocks up the street, of Vilna's largest synagogue. My uncle Lyova, a distinguished physician, was a stern, taciturn man with a small mustache, but his wife, Dora, a teacher, overflowed with warmth, as did my grandmother, a tiny woman always wearing a kerchief. My nine-year old cousin, Sarah, was shy but friendly, except when something or other would make her pout with resentment. As time went on, it was I who brought on some of these occasional moods, by teasing Sarah about her French lessons (her parents decided early on that she, as a member of a good Jewish-Russian intelligentsia family, should learn French), or about her piano playing when, poor thing, she was forced to practice a Clementi or Czerny sonatina in my presence. My reputation as a *lobuz* (prankster) preceded me, and what amused me felt like torture to her. But it took me some years to understand that.

The center of social and intellectual activity in the Pomerantz apartment (our home, as it would turn out, for over a year) was the living room/dining room, with a sturdy table in the middle, on which rested majestically a large samovar. Heated by coal, the samovar gurgled from morning to night (a Polish maid attended to it), so it was always possible to help oneself to a glass of tea, with a lump of sugar or *varenie* (preserves, Russian, usually made from strawberries). My father would sometimes be absent in the evening: though police stations were still manned by Polish policemen, as were the telephone lines and other municipal services, Soviet troops held control of the city, which dictated a continuous change of sleeping arrangements. After a while, I learned never to inquire as to his nocturnal whereabouts. (The petrifying knock at the door announcing the presence of the authorities invariably took place after midnight. A popular joke had it that a family is woken up in the middle of the night by a knock at the door, only to be reassured by a neighbor, "Don't worry, citizens, it's only a fire!")

This ever-present menace hanging over our heads no doubt affected the adults more than me and my friends. I fell in love with Vilna: its many baroque and Renaissance churches; the old university; the Jewish quarter with its narrow, winding streets, including the Jewish Street (a name that persisted until the Germans liquidated the Vilna Ghetto in 1944); the Straszun Library, founded in 1892, one of the oldest Jewish libraries in Eastern Europe. The *shulhoyf* (synagogue courtyard) contained the headquarters of all the community's religious and secular organizations, as well as the synagogue of the great Enlightenment rabbi known as the "Vilna Gaon," whose stress on the study of the Talmud, philosophy and mathematics and whose vehement opposition to the charismatic and miracle-worshiping Chassidim dominated Jewish life in Vilna from the late 18th century onward.

Vilna was a handsome city set in a handsome locality. The river Wilia flows through it, as does another narrow stream, the Wilejka. The ruins of the castle of the early 14th century Grand Duke of Lithuania, Gedymin, overlooks the city, its hillside a favorite place of young couples seeking some privacy. The city was then surrounded by spruce forests, and in the summer kayaks and swimmers crowded both rivers.

But the place I fell most in love with was the *real* [two syllables: re-al] *gimnazye*, one of the few high schools with Yiddish as its language of instruction. All the pupils spoke Yiddish (the *litvak* Yiddish which was closer to me than the Warsaw dialect), as did the teaching staff. My parents signed me up at the *gimnazye* a few days after we arrived in Vilna. Classes were in disarray, what with no one knowing exactly whom Vilna now belonged to and what changes - if any - would be made in our curriculum. The situation was tailor-made for my rambunctious proclivities. Within a few days, I found a classroom containing a piano, and invited a number of boys to join me in a new chorus - to be called, I announced grandly, the New Real Gimnazye Choir. I taught them the Polish revolutionary march I'd learned in Warsaw, *Nasze kiszki marsza grają*, and an indecent song in Yiddish - God only knows where I had learned it - about a rabbi with a prominent sex organ. News about my initiative soon reached the proper authorities, and I was called into the principal's office and read a stern lecture never to engage in such scandalous activities again. My singing mates, like myself, were dismayed but not altogether surprised by this development.

The chaos raging in the *real gimnazye* - as for that matter in the whole city - did not last long, for on October 20, a few weeks after the Red Army occupied Vilna, the Soviet troops quietly moved out of the city, and a new military force took over: that of the Lithuanian Republic. This, we learned just the night before, was part of an agreement - now made public - whereby Vilna was ceded to Lithuania in exchange for several thousand Russian troops to be stationed throughout the country.

Virtually the entire population of Vilna, or so it seemed to me, gathered that morning on the banks of the Wilia to await (and meekly applaud) the new troops. It was a bizarre sight, and for some of the elderly residents of Vilna, who had lived through the two tumultuous years (1918-1920) when Vilna was part of the new post-World War I Lithuanian Republic, grandly amusing: miniscule tanks; strapping young men, each of them (by regulation, as we found out) one meter 80cm (about six feet) tall, in resplendent uniforms and high fur caps; equally impressively attired cavalry detachments.

To us youngsters, for whom Lithuania, despite its role in the history of Vilna, was an almost mythical entity, it all seemed like a comic-opera spectacle, to which we reacted with giggles, luckily not audible to the solemn-faced members of the Lithuanian armed forces. After the troops passed, we went home, to find that among some of Vilna's Polish residents the arrival of the Lithuanians aroused not so much amusement as an appetite for a little pogrom. Why not? No doubt the Jews were responsible for the calamitous events of the past few weeks, with Poland invaded by Germans and Russians and Wilno – in the Polish spelling - ceded to Poland's enemy in the north, weren't they? So they had it coming to them. I remember standing next to my aunt looking out on the street where gangs of teenage boys were shouting and making threatening gestures. Suddenly one of them picked up a rock and threw it at our window; others followed suit.

Luckily my aunt had the presence of mind to snap closed the inside shutters, so the splintered glass caused no harm to anyone. My uncle, livid with anger, grabbed the phone and called the closest police station to demand immediate action. Fortunately the young hoodlums soon dispersed. A small tank (!) pulled up to the front of our house only an hour later, by which time life on the street had resumed its everyday routine.

A period of quasi-normalcy now ensued. Political parties and organizations reemerged from the shadows, newspapers in several languages draped the kiosks, and my father, who found a job at Vilna's Central Educational Committee, headquarters of the Yiddish secular schools, began to spend his nights at home. The Lithuanian policemen spoke their incomprehensible language, but some of them also knew Polish and Russian, so communication proved not much of a problem. Dairy products and staples filled the stores and old familiar restaurants again catered to a clientele grateful to pick up the ordinary routines of life.

At the *real gimnazye*, the transition to a modified curriculum went fairly smoothly. Polish and Polish history went out the door, and in their place came something called Lithuanian and Lithuanian history, subjects we thought bizarre and funny but which we (meaning the usually rowdy pupils) decided to tolerate *faute de mieux*.

In April the school commemorated the 25th anniversary of the death of one of the giants of Yiddish literature, Itzhak Leib Peretz (1852-1915). At the ceremony, I was required to recite from memory one of Peretz's more abstruse tales, which I did not even begin to understand. My teacher, a portly man with a goatee, Yankev Gershteyn, a fanatical Yiddishist who refused to speak to any Jews in any other language, and who also conducted a choir that was to continue to perform in the Ghetto, stubbornly insisted that I learn the story by heart, whether I liked it or not. And so, for seemingly interminable days, after classes were over, I would traipse to an empty classroom, there to rehearse the incomprehensible lines under Gershteyn's stern gaze. When the day of the commemoration arrived, my performance proved a delight to the adult audience, and a total bore to my fellow students. Still, my thespian tendencies received another jolt of encouragement.

Otherwise, life proceeded uneventfully. As long, that is, that you did not have to worry about the future. But how to avoid worrying? By the spring of 1940 rumors swept Vilna that the current political arrangements might be short-lived and that the Soviets were considering reoccupying Lithuania. Needless to say such gossip only served to generate stressful days and sleepless nights, not in the least assuaged by the absence of solid, reliable information. (The short-wave radio stations of distant capitals, from Stockholm to London, also seemed to deal more in rumors than in facts.) Nevertheless, my father and fellow-Bundists began to discuss the possibilities of getting out of Lithuania should the worst-case scenario come to pass. (These conversations took place out of my earshot but judging from the nervous tension they produced it was not difficult to figure out what they were about.) One idea, I learned later, was to get a boat that would take us to Sweden... It was quickly vetoed.

Among my schoolmates the mood was no jollier. The only exception was one of my closest friends, a short bespectacled boy with a crewcut, who spoke several languages, including English taught him - so he claimed - by his one-time English nanny. (When I first met him, he was reading Tolstoy's *War and Peace* in Russian.) Mark told me his parents assured him nothing untoward was going to happen, since the Soviet Union would not allow any harm to come to the "masses." (Mark's parents were Communists, despite their decidedly bourgeois lifestyle.) I liked Mark - in fact I was quite impressed with him - but I could not share his fervent ideological optimism.

The day that almost everyone expected came in early June, when Lithuanian troops suddenly made themselves scarce and Red Army soldiers again appeared on the streets of Vilna. The change in atmosphere became almost palpable. Political organizations and institutions, until now functioning freely, ground to a halt. People like my father again had to seek shelter at night, not sure whether the Soviet secret police was back on the job. Above all there was anxiety about the future: if the Soviets take over, what then?

On June 15 the announcement came: the Soviet Union had come to an agreement with the three Baltic states, Lithuania, Latvia, and Estonia. Their populations would vote on whether they approved joining the USSR. Knowing what we did about the Moscow's respect for democratic norms, we had few doubts about the outcome of the plebiscites. On the day of the vote my parents and I were in Kaunas, capital of Lithuania. I watched through the hotel window as Russian soldiers knocked at the doors of private homes and apartments to remind their occupants of their civic duty. It was a weird sight, embarrassingly transparent in its hypocrisy.

The next day, the results were made public: about 98 percent of all Estonians, Latvians, and Lithuanians voted for joining the socialist motherland. The USSR Supreme Soviet, the "parliament" of the country, swiftly voted its approval and so in less than a day three new "constituent republics" joined the USSR: numbers 14, 15 and 16. The former parliaments of those countries voted to dissolve themselves. It was all remarkably efficient.

For me the most dramatic changes took place in the *real gimnazye*. The history of the USSR immediately replaced Lithuanian history. Yiddish literature was gradually shorn of its "bourgeois" writers, save the three major writers of the 19th century, Mendele Moikher Sforim, Itzhak Peretz and Sholem Aleichem, all three of whom were declared to have been essentially "progressive" and pro-socialist. (In fact Sholem Aleichem had become the most widely published Yiddish writer in the Soviet Union.) In the two-plus decades of its existence, the new Russia had not quite managed to raise a generation of writers fully versed in the art of "socialist realism," but it boasted a number of Yiddish poets, some of them very good, approved by the authorities – although many of them repeatedly got into hot water by writing something deemed "nationalistic" or "bourgeois" or "individualistic" by the guardians of the official literary canon.

Our languages program became even more complex. Yiddish of course stayed. So did Lithuanian, as the official language of the (now "socialist") republic, to which was added Russian, language of the state. In addition, as if these were not "foreign" enough, we were also required to take English as a "foreign language." (Our teacher, the wife of a Bundist, had flaming red hair and a penchant for infectious laughter, which substantially mitigated our resentment.) How we were to deal with this linguistic embarrassment of riches? Russian did not prove to be much of a problem, especially for the natives of Vilna. English was interesting. Lithuanian, however, continued to be a steady source of bile and ill humor.

The severest shock for me personally was the sudden conversion of almost all of my classmates – good friends until then – into ardent Communists who eagerly joined the new "Red Pioneer" organization. Apparently I was the only one in my class still bearing the old torch. All the others enthusiastically endorsed the wave of the future.

This became painfully obvious at a literature class, where we were all required to read a poem by Itzik Feffer, one of the more sycophantic Soviet Yiddish poets. Called "Ode to Khaver (comrade) Stalin", it contained perhaps forty stanzas. When my turn came, I read:

er iz tifer fun di yamen, er iz hekher fun di berg
nokh aza iz nit faranen oyf der kaylekhdiker erd.
("He is deeper than the oceans/ He is taller than all peaks/ There is simply no one like him/ On our round earth.")

Apparently I read these embarrassing lines without requisite passion, for the students – all my erstwhile friends! - began to hiss: "Make him read it again, teacher! He can do better than that!" The teacher, whom I knew to be a Bund sympathizer, turned to me and said, using my nickname: "Amik, do please read it again. With more feeling." Which I did. Never did I hate my fellow-students more than on that day. I now understood what terror, without physical force, meant.

An equally painful and politically enlightening incident concerned a play all students in the *gimnazye* were required to attend. The play revolved around a 21-year old Bundist worker, Hirsh Lekert, who in May 1902 fired several shots at the Tsarist governor of Vilna, General Viktor von Wahl, in reprisal for the public flogging of 20 Jewish and six Polish workers found guilty of organizing a May Day demonstration. Though the bullets inflicted little harm, Lekert was brought before a military tribunal and hanged several days later. His execution sparked a series of violent protests in Vilna and in other Russian cities. Overnight, he became a folk hero, a symbol of resistance to brutal tyranny, a martyr and the subject of songs, plays and commemorations for years to come.

The Bund did not fully approve of Lekert's act: Marxist parties disapproved of individual terrorism as a potentially harmful method of political struggle, preferring mass action. Still, the Bund did not condemn Lekert, interpreting his act as one of self-defense and as a vindication of "revolutionary honor".

Not so the Communists. In the play we saw, the Bund had been transformed into an ally of the Tsarist regime, a traitor to the proletariat, Jewish and non-Jewish alike. A group of seedy-looking Bundists plead with Lekert - presumably a dedicated Bolshevik - to desist. When he refused, they denounced him to the *Okhrana* (Tsarist secret police.)

So many years after the event, I still remember my anguish at this play. I realized I should not simply accept the contents of the play on faith. Nevertheless I wondered about the accuracy of the Bund's version, with which I had grown up. In torment, I turned to my father for an explanation. The Soviet Union, said my father, was turning history upside down: all Communists were presented as upstanding revolutionaries, all their opponents as vile cowards and traitors. My doubts, said my father soothingly, were understandable, for to whom could young people turn for guidance when so many people were afraid to speak their minds? The Lekert play, he said, was a prime example of this Bolshevik falsification of history. In the future, I had plenty of opportunities to recall my father's words.

Life in those days was not all tension and upheaval. Comedy, or at least quasi-comedy, played its part as well. On November 7, 1940, for instance, all students of the *real gimnazye* were ordered to join the populace of Vilna marching through the streets in honor of the twenty-third anniversary of the October (November) 1917 Revolution. We were instructed to shout, in whatever language we preferred, "Long live the mighty Soviet Union!" and "Long live Comrade Stalin!" (*zol lebn der mekhtiker ratnfarband; zol lebn der khaver Stalin*). From time to time, in the midst of all the jubilation, and after making sure that no one could hear me, I mischievously substituted my own name for Stalin's: after all, November 7 was my holiday, too - namely, my 14th birthday! Of course, I didn't dream of sharing this very private information with any of my co-marchers... When I came home, my mother served me a cup of hot cocoa and a French pastry from a nearby patisserie, a fine reward for having held my tongue.

I had to be discreet about other matters, too. My father had long since applied for an exit visa, transit visas from the Japanese and Dutch consulates, and a visa to go to the United States. Eventually he received them, thanks to Chiune Sugihara, the Japanese vice consul in Kaunas. In tandem with Jan Zwarterndijk, a Dutch diplomat, Sugihara enabled some 2000 Polish Jews to leave the Soviet Union in 1940-1941.[2] How could the Soviet Union grant permission to my father and others to leave Soviet territory, while at the same time these same individuals, should they be recognized (or denounced) as Bundists, could at any moment be arrested? This is something I cannot satisfactorily explain, except to note that these were bizarre times, and during such times extraordinary and bizarre things do happen.

Accordingly, my father and other Jews took the risk and approached the various consulates. They did so before Lithuania "joined" the Soviet Union. Which explains why my father and I were in Kaunas on June 15 when the Lithuanian masses, with some help from the Red Army, went to the polls. Shortly thereafter, the Kaunas headquarters of the MVD (Ministry of Internal Affairs) became one more office to visit in search of approval to leave the country: that is, a Soviet exit visa.

To lessen the risk of running into a Communist who would recognize him and promptly denounce him as a "class enemy," my father rented a small apartment in a town about 50 kilometers from Kaunas. He shared the flat with another Bundist, Shlomo Gilinsky, the head of the Medem Sanatorium's bureau in Warsaw, who had (like my father) succeeded in leaving the capital at the outbreak of the war, together with his wife and son. There the two men lived, under assumed names, while they waited for their visas to materialize.

My mother and I visited them only once, in July. The situation was grotesque, made more so by the fact that both men would regularly enter the enemy's maw - the MVD office - to inquire about the progress of the visa applications for which they had applied *under their own names*! Later on, when I tried to make head or tail out of it, I was told that the various Soviet offices were at that time in such a state of confusion that the right hand did not know what the left one was doing. As the Yiddish saying goes, *fun dayn moyl in gots oyern* (from your mouth into God's ears). At any rate, the confusion, if that's what it was, served us well.

In addition to my mother and me, my father resolved to take one more person under his wing and added to the family a young man, ostensibly his son by an earlier marriage. This altogether fictitious scheme involved all sorts of dangerous procedures such as changing my father's passport and obtaining a false birth certificate for my "half brother," in order to bring the new "Harry Brumberg" (né Hirzhbeyn) to the United Sates where his sweetheart was waiting for him.

What persuaded my father to take such a risk? For one thing, Hirzhbeyn had worked as a secretary to my father at the sanatorium. Second, he was an orphan, without any means of support. Finally, it so happened that his girl friend had once been hired by my parents as a "mother's helper', and had won my mother's heart. Other considerations apart, my father's innate kindness made him embark on this extremely dangerous step. As it happens, the ruse was not detected, and my half-brother landed in the arms of his wife-to-be without a mishap. In America, where he became a traveling salesman, I lost track of him, though I did meet him once, several years later, and found to my astonishment that "Harry Brumberg" had entirely lost his Yiddish and Polish, replacing them with a fairly rudimentary English. His wife Reginka (diminutive for Regina) bore him three children, and kept up a relationship with my mother for several years, but eventually she, too, disappeared from sight.

We managed to bring Hirzhbeyn with us, but not our family, and the thought of our relatives remaining behind as we got ready to depart from Vilna was sheer torment to my parents. There was no choice. Politically, my father was at a greater risk of being arrested than anyone else in his family; the sooner he left the better. Moreover, as Polish citizens – if only nominally - we could legally apply for departure, while the Pomerantzes, now Soviet citizens, could not. Dora and Lyova urged my parents not to feel guilty. They would, they assured him, eventually join us in New York. It didn't work out quite that way. My grandmother died before the Nazis entered Vilna. The Nazis sent my uncle to an extermination camp, and Dora and Sarah to a work camp, which they barely survived. We managed to bring them into Sweden, and, in 1947, to the United States.

In December 1940 the visas came through. My father informed us he would take a train in Kaunas that would stop in Vilna, where we were to join him. Then we would all go on to Moscow. Naturally, I was instructed to inform no one of our plans.

And so early in January, I vaulted down the staircase leading into the schoolyard. I bid my friends a casual good-bye, as if it were just another school day, as if I'd see them the next morning, as if everything was normal. It was a horrible, brutal afternoon. A few hours later, we went to the train station. My father, who had embarked in Kaunas, stepped off the train, embraced his sister, mother, brother-in-law, niece. No one said a word. Then a whistle blew. The train shuddered. We were on our way.

5

The Great Adventure: Part One

*To Moscow. A Guided Tour. By Train Through Siberia.
A Whiff of Birobidjan. Farewell Russia!*

Wrapped in thought, we sat silently as our train pulled out of the Vilna railroad station, then gradually picked up speed. My parents must have been wondering anxiously whether they would ever be reunited with their family. So was I. In addition, I felt sick about the make-believe scene earlier that day, when I bid a merry adieu to all my unsuspecting friends in my school's spacious courtyard, knowing that I would not see them the following day - if ever.

(In the spring of 2001, during a brief stay in Vilna with a film crew from Germany, I walked over to the same courtyard. The *gimnazye* happened to be one of the few surviving buildings of the Vilna Ghetto, where it had served as headquarters for the Judenrat, the "Jewish Council" whose officials were forced to collaborate with their German masters in rounding up the remaining Vilna Jews for deportation and death. I recounted, in front of a camera, the story of my departure from this very spot more than half a century earlier. It was an eerie feeling.)

We arrived at the Belorusskii train station in Moscow in the morning. By that time I was mildly excited and certainly curious about what lay ahead. In a way that even I, at the age of 14, understood, the departure from Vilna marked an end of one phase in our lives and the beginning of another. From now on, we ceased to be mere victims of fate; for the first time in many months we felt at least partially in charge of our lives and of our future. For a teen-aged boy it was the start of a Great Adventure.

Moscow's Belorusskii station was teeming with the most wretched mass of humanity I had ever seen. People covered in rags were sprawled on every surface – benches, the ground, one another; bundles of gristly, fatty sausages wrapped in newspapers jostled against bread and bottles. Everywhere children ran to and fro, relieving themselves on the platform, while the adults looked on with indifference. As usual in such circumstances, I turned to my father for an explanation of this extraordinary scene. My father - a man of the world, after all, and a one-time resident of Moscow - explained that in Russia passengers sometimes had to spend several days at a station waiting for a train to take them to their next destination. Having a ticket - assuming you could purchase one - meant little. You never knew when your train would arrive. And so the railroad station became your temporary abode – sleeping quarters, privy and kitchen combined. He had left Russia more than twenty years ago, but the present seemed no different from the past... A few minutes later, we piled into a rickety taxi, and my father, in his impeccable Russian, told the driver the name of the hotel where reservations had been made for us by Intourist.

The hotel, called Novaya Moskovskaya Gostinitsa (New Moscow Hotel), perched on an embankment of the Moscow River, across from the Kremlin. It was a shabby building, though fabulous to me. That night we had our meal in the hotel's luxury dining room on the 12th floor, though I don't remember why. We drank from crystal goblets while a gypsy ensemble performed, weaving its way through the tables of animated diners. My mother, in honor of this occasion, let me drink a glass of wine. Cloud nine!

In the following days, we dined in the hotel's main dining room on the ground floor, in far less opulent surroundings, where the food was mediocre at best and where no gypsies entertained the diners. In the lobby, my father commended to my attention what he termed an example of "an essential truth about the Soviet Union." A large plaque in front of the elevator proclaimed in bold letters: "WORKERS! USE THE ELEVATOR!" Below, a much smaller notice announced: "The elevator is out of order." (*RABOCHIE: UPOTRE-BLIAITE LIFT! ... Lift ne rabotaet*)

(Many years later, when I came to Moscow in my capacity as an employee of the United States Information Agency, I met with a young Russian woman I had befriended on one of my previous visits to the Soviet Union. I was staying in the Ukraina Hotel, a hotel for foreigners, while she had a room in the Novaya Moskovskaya, now called Hotel Bucharest and reserved for Soviet citizens. She showed me her room - small and dingy - and then her bathroom, so that I would "understand something about the Soviet Union." It was huge, and entirely empty except for its [seatless] toilet.)

My parents, I felt, were as excited as I was, though in my father's case sadness must have marred his excitement. He had graduated from a Tsarist gymnasium in Moscow on the eve of the Revolution and knew the city well. (Some years ago, I came across his diploma: he was, I discovered with pride, an *otlichnik*, a straight A-student.) And he still had some relatives living in Moscow. He knew their addresses, but he dared not visit or call them. Under High Stalinism, contacts between Soviets and foreigners - especially those with such dangerous credentials as my father's - could be punished by imprisonment, *ssylka* (exile) or *katorga* (hard labor). He could not put them at such risk. My mother and I saw the sights of Moscow with my father acting as guide. The expenses were minimal, and we had enough rubles. We paid a visit to the grand Tretiakov Gallery, admired the vastness of Red Square, got tickets to the fabled Moscow Circus and the Bolshoi Opera. At the latter, we saw a performance of Glinka's ballet "The Hunchbacked Horse" (*Koniok Garbunok*), and were spellbound by the brilliant lights, the costumes, the lavish scenery, the dancers dressed in peasant costumes, the ebullient music. I remember sitting next to several other children in the last row of the third balcony, our heads almost touching the vaulted ceiling. We craned our necks and wondered excitedly whether the dancer far off on the distant stage, naked to the waist, was a man or a woman. (We never found out, but this being Moscow, not Paris, it is not difficult to guess.)

Good tourists, we decided to go to the Lenin Mausoleum. We had to wait in the long line of visitors for about an hour, inching our way forward until we reached the gate of the small building; on each side stood rigidly a Red Army soldier, with fur-cap and raised bayonet. After doffing our hats, we entered, moving slowly along with the others. When we came to the bier shielded by thick glass, we stole a glance at Lenin's pasty face. So there he was, the one-time father of the Soviet Union and leader of the world proletariat, the man who ordered the shooting of hundreds of anti-Bolshevik peasants and other sworn Enemies of the Socialist State, now being mutely examined by a queue of people warned sternly by the guards not to linger, not to get lost in thought but to move, move, move. It was a bizarre experience - worthwhile, perhaps, but one I was relieved to put out of my mind as soon as we emerged again into the cold Moscow air.

All told, Moscow was overwhelming. Trolleys, busses and trucks filled the streets, as did huge crowds of scruffily dressed people, some (this in January!) wearing sandals, walking as fast as they could through the wind and slush. The shop-windows displayed everything from women's dresses to caviar, but the shelves inside stood half empty: yet another startling contrast between appearance and reality. After five days the time came to board the Trans-Siberian train that in less than two weeks would deposit us in Vladivostok, whence we were to proceed by boat to Japan. Just as our train was pulling out of the railway station, we froze: a long string of freight cars packed to the brim with hundreds of men and women stood on an adjacent track. Since rifle-carrying soldiers surrounded the cars, there could be no doubt who the "passengers" were and where they were heading. We stared, mouths agape, at the sight. The Soviets citizens on our train paid it no attention.

Our section of the train, divided into compartments containing four sleeping bunks each, was occupied almost entirely by Polish-Jewish refugees; Soviet passengers rode in separate cars. There was a dining car where we were assigned seats at specified times, each meal paid for with a coupon provided by Intourist. There we chatted with other Bundists. All of us found our presence on this train, rather than on the kind bound for Siberia or Arctic labor camps, little short of a miracle. At the end of each car sat a woman, her head wrapped in the standard kerchief, attending to a samovar filled with *kipiatok* (boiling water) and a small teapot with *zavarka* (essence of tea). When the *zavarka* ran out, passengers were expected to produce their own tea leaves, which many had purchased in Moscow.

For days the landscape was unrelievedly bleak. Ice and snow covered empty fields, the vista occasionally broken by a few dilapidated and shabby peasant huts. Three times a day the train would stop at some desolate station where our tea-ladies filled up their samovars. Time permitting, we could don our overcoats and rush onto the platform to buy an ice cream bar. It was an incongruous notion in the middle of a Russian winter, but Russians of all ages love ice cream no matter what the season, and we were glad of the break. A visit to the snow-swept station afforded a rare opportunity to stretch one's legs while enjoying a tasty treat into the bargain.

A Chassidic family of five occupied the compartment next to ours. My parents were particularly taken with one of the three children, a boy of about nine, with long sidelocks and an earnest face, whom they once enticed into our compartment. Warsaw, of course, had been full of these Orthodox black-clad Chassidim, dressed in long coats, the men with beards, the women bewigged or with kerchiefs covering their heads. I often saw them on the streets, but they kept to themselves, and I never talked with any of them. Now I listened attentively as my parents conversed with the boy about where he lived, whether he had his own bed or slept with his mother, and how his father made a living. The boy remained unperturbed, explaining gravely that *"fin der haym trugt men kayn soydes nisht aroys"* (loosely, "family matters are private"). My father, an entirely secular man whose professional life had long been involved with children, found the boy's reticence enchanting. "You see", he told us afterwards, "here you have the clue to a good upbringing." Having grown up with the image of a Chassid as little more than a fanatic steeped in obscurantist lore, I was amazed at my father's tolerant approval.

A week after we left Moscow, we approached the shores of Lake Baikal. Everybody rose at five o'clock that morning, and, fortified with a glass of tea, stood or sat glued to the window, gazing out at the dark blue water of the enormous lake. I don't remember seeing any boats, but then, this was winter, and the temperature must have been at least minus thirty centigrade. Baikal's size astonished me: for most of an entire day the train hurtled in and out of tunnels along the shoreline, billowing smoke and piercing the air with its powerful whistle.

Shortly before arriving in Vladivostok, the train stopped at a small station, Londoko. The name was spelled out in both Cyrillic and Yiddish lettering. We had entered the territory of the Birobidjan Autonomous Jewish Region, established in 1930 as part of an effort to strengthen the security of the Soviet Union and to provide a counterweight to the lure of Zionism still strong among many Soviet Jews. The experiment did not prove much of a success. Most of the immigrants left the area soon after arrival, disillusioned by the harsh climate, the swamps, swarms of voracious insects, absence of roads, and lack of elementary living accommodations. By 1941, only 20,000 Jews remained in Birobidjan, out of a total of 180,000 inhabitants. (By now there are virtually no Jews left there.)

Ours, as we later learned, was the first of the several trainloads of Jewish-Polish refugees to pull into this village of which none of us had ever heard. Previous trainloads had stopped in the capital of Birobidjan, where they had been besieged by hundreds, perhaps thousands, of Jews carrying letters to their relatives and friends in the United States, and not averse to pouring out their hearts to fellow Jews. This was clearly undesirable: to the authorities, a small village, with hardly anyone at the station, seemed preferable.

With half an hour to go before leaving the station, my parents and a few other people disembarked and began to pace the platform. They stopped to talk to a young man of about eighteen, one of the few people on the platform, wearing long boots and a fur-lined jacket. I later found out that they carefully avoided asking any political questions, querying him about matters like the price of bread and potatoes. But then what was not political at that time? After a few minutes, two uniformed men appeared. One put his hand on the young man's right shoulder, the other on his left, and with a gruff "let's go, comrade," they led him away. My parents were horror-stricken. At best we hoped the young man got no more than a stern reprimand, though one he was not likely to forget... On the twelfth day of our journey, the train chugged into the poorly-lit station of Vladivostok, and several NKVD soldiers whisked us away to be searched, scrutinizing our passports and visas with particular care. Our boat to Japan was to leave later that night. I remember little of our stay at the police station, except that one uniformed man told me to step into a side room and undress to my underwear. He searched me thoroughly: apparently, something about my appearance aroused his suspicion. Not finding any *valiuta* (hard currency) or valuables either on my body or among my clothes, he told me to get dressed and join my anxious parents. (My father had, in fact, $300 sewn into the sole of his left shoe. It went undetected.)

And so, after this last encounter with Soviet security, we climbed a wobbly gangplank resting against an ill-smelling Japanese vessel used to transport cattle. It contained no cabins, only large open compartments, their floors covered with sawdust. But who cared? Liberation beckoned. Moments later everyone gathered on the deck, and watched as an ice-breaker steered the boat through massive clumps of ice into the open sea.

When we finally pulled out of Soviet territorial waters and the huge red star illuminating the harbor began to fade into the distance, pandemonium broke loose. Laughter, weeping, singing swelled into one huge roar. Freedom at last! I suspect that few of us stopped to think of what might be awaiting those they had left behind, or for that matter what lay ahead for ourselves. For the time being, exultation crowded out all other emotions. It was enough.

6

The Great Adventure: Part Two

A Fairy Tale Called Japan. The Delights of Kobe. Yokohama and the US Consulate. The Asama Maru. My First Seduction. America!

The nighttime passage from Vladivostok was brief but grueling. Most of the passengers lay on the floor, wrapped in their coats and thin blankets, unable to sleep most of the time, quietly groaning as the sea surged and the boat lurched violently from one side to the other. There was nothing to do but suffer in silence. My father and several other men, as if eager to display their machismo, refused to lie down and spent a good part of the night on the deck, only occasionally stepping downstairs for relief from the punishing cold and drizzle. The pleas of my mother and others to the men to remain downstairs were of no avail. For those men the action, such as it was, was on the deck.

As arrows of sunshine began to penetrate our sleeping quarters and the boat ceased to sway, everyone took to the deck. Overnight, winter had turned into spring. The sea was placid, the air tepid, a mild breeze was caressing our faces. Soon, the first Japanese islands came into sight, covered with lush vegetation and flowers.

The Japanese sailors, all smiles and no communication, distributed cups of tea with lemon and dry rolls. Our excitement grew as the boat began to pull into a port, its whistle piercing the air, the sailors straining at the ropes, the children huddling around their parents. Soon, the boat came to a halt, a gangplank was lowered from the deck and we began to descend upon it cautiously until we felt the firm ground under our feet. With the exception of small bags, our luggage was being lowered from the boat in huge nets, which were then emptied onto the ground. We looked around, full of excitement. A new chapter in the Great Adventure was about to begin.

Tsuruga - the port – looked tiny to us; so did everything else around us. A train was waiting for us a hundred yards from the boat, more a toy train, it seemed to us, than a real one. The trees were shorter than the ones we were used to, and the Japanese scurrying to and fro, men in dark robes, women in colorful kimonos, were also uniformly short and slight. A tiny make-believe world - a fairy tale.

The two months between our arrival in Japan and our departure for the United States in May 1941 were for me pure enchantment. The train took us from Tsuruga to Kobe, a day's trip, which we spent eyeing the passing countryside, and sustaining ourselves on sandwiches and tea available at the dining car (if memory serves, we had some dollars on us). The Japanese were infallibly polite and helpful, though we could exchange not a single word.

Once in Kobe, we settled in a small but comfortable apartment in a small house on a quiet street lined with cherry trees. The kitchen was spacious, with plenty of pots, pans, plates and cutlery, and the two bedrooms were equipped with blankets and colorful quilts. The bathroom had a shower - sheer luxury!

On our coffee table we spotted several brochures in English about Kobe and surroundings, which we studied avidly. Several other Polish-Jewish families moved into apartments in the same house, and near-by, some with children my age. And so the following day we proceeded to wander, my friends and I, through the city, visited temples and sacred gardens where deer wandered around freely. Once my family took a train to Tokyo, where we admired the Ginza commercial district - no longer Japan in miniature - with its wide streets, restaurants, shops and the first department stores I had ever seen. We parked ourselves in a teahouse and drank cups of tea, sitting cross-legged on soft cushions.

We went to a six-hour spectacle, a mixture of cinema, ballet and other forms of entertainment, which family groups watched, sprawled on blankets and consuming, it seemed to us, unending quantities of food - rice, vegetables and unidentifiable viands which they brought with them in large picnic baskets. The film was of course in Japanese and all the parts were read by a single person sitting in a booth in front of the screen. Among the exciting amusements offered were sumo wrestling matches, which everybody watched in absolute silence. The enormous athletes, sweat pouring from their blubbery bodies, clasped each other in brutal embraces, ending each match with one of the two thrown to the ground. Jerzy, a boy of about seventeen sitting next to me, one of our group of Bundists, whispered to me during one of the intermissions: "Each one of these wrestlers had three average Japanese for breakfast this morning." Jerzy had a peculiar sense of humor...

In the outskirts of Kobe, I would take daily walks with another boy, Henry. We would hike for hours through the hilly roads surrounding the city, where kimono-clad Japanese would rush out of their houses to stare at us, apparently unused to seeing anyone with non-Oriental features. I relished those walks, the undulating hills covered with a variety of fruit trees, all in bloom, the marvelous sensation of freedom and absence of any responsibility.

Another time I went with a friend to a Japanese bath, which we heard was quite spectacular. It was divided into a men's section, and a women's section, where people disrobed and, fetching small bowls, filled them with hot (or very hot) water, took a bar of soap and proceeded to wash themselves thoroughly. After that, you stepped into one of the communal pools, choosing one with water at a reasonable temperature. The water in some of the pools seemed to be close to boiling; I couldn't understand how anyone could stand it, but some remained in it for a long time. Incidentally, during these proceedings women bath attendants moved around, distributing bowls, towels and white robes. Nobody paid them the slightest attention.

After one month we moved to Yokohama, as did many of our friends, in order to be closer to the American Embassy where we hoped to get our visas. The daily wait for news from the embassy was nerve-racking, made no less so by our anxieties about the relatives and friends we left behind. My mother's mother and other close relatives, we learned later, stayed in Warsaw, in the Ghetto. I had no courage to imagine what their final weeks were like; but the books on the ghetto I came to devour later on, as well as Roman Polanski's film *The Pianist*, eventually supplied some of the unspeakable details. All my mother's family, with the exception of one brother, perished in Treblinka.

I was particularly impressed by my father's occasional telephone calls to the United States from a booth in our apartment house in Yokohama. Imagine: go into a booth, say something over the telephone and presto - you are speaking to the United States! I was also proud that he had been delegated as spokesman for the entire group of comrades. Most of my parents' friends received their visas quickly. Others, less fortunate, were not able to get their visas on time, and after Japan bombed Pearl Harbor in December 1941 they were sent to Shanghai (already housing a good number of Jewish refugees, mostly from Germany). We were lucky. After a month, the visas finally arrived. Our relief was indescribable. We had all fallen in love with Japan, but couldn't wait to leave it.

Our boat, *Asama Maru*, left Yokohama on April 27. We were to spend nearly two weeks on it, and I was brimming with excitement. *Asama Maru* was nothing like the wretched cattle boat on which we had crossed the Sea of Japan. It was, I found out later, the last Japanese boat setting out on a peaceful mission before Pearl Harbor. The voyage was interrupted once by an 18-hour stopover in Honolulu. Among the passengers were Japanese, Americans, and a sprinkling of Europeans, but the bulk were Polish-Jewish refugees.

A motley crowd filled the decks and cabins of *Asama Maru*. In the first class section, inaccessible to me, were the nabobs, speaking English, German, French and Japanese. On the second deck, in addition to Japanese and English, you heard mostly Polish and some Yiddish, and on the third the reverse - Yiddish with a dash of Polish. Which subtly reflected the social differences between these two groups of refugees: the largely assimilated Jewish bourgeoisie on the second deck, the stalwart proletarians and intellectuals below. Dubbed *folks-inteligentsye* in Yiddish ("people's intelligentsia"), the latter included Zionists, Labor Zionists, Mizrakhi (religious Zionists), and Bundists.

The boat trip entranced me from first to last. I loved the huge dining room, where white-jacketed waiters moved adroitly between the tables filling the wineglasses of my grown-up companions. I loved the deck with its sun-worshippers reclining in chaise-lounges while other passengers crowded around the single shuffleboard court and the three ping-pong tables. I loved, too, the sparkling Pacific stretching into the distance. At night in our cabin I would ensconce myself in my bunk, engrossed in a Conan Doyle novel, and then sink into sleep, not waking until morning.

I spent most of my days with several Bundist youngsters, ages 10 to 13; we regaled one another with stories of our experiences under the Soviet regime in Vilna, played inane games and made irreverent comments about our fellow-passengers. One member of the group was a tall, lanky ten-year-old girl named Halina Joelson, daughter of a tall, lanky father and a short, lumpy mother, both Bundists. Halina (or in the diminutive, Halinka), I decided, was one of the most beautiful creatures I had ever laid eyes on. She had long brown hair plaited in thick braids, lovely smooth skin, a small nose, and an air of sublime innocence that drove me, a teenager in the throes of puberty, mad with desire. I could not keep my eyes off her, and asked my parents to arrange for her family to eat at our table, which they did.

This might have been as close as I got to Halina, were it not for one fortuitous occurrence. The boat boasted a swimming pool open only to first- and second-class passengers. I yearned to try it, if possible with the girl of my dreams. But how? Luckily, there was a passenger in the second class, one Szereszewski, a portly man, nattily dressed and always sporting a long, elegant holder with an unlit cigarette in it. Despite his middle class background and Zionist convictions (I think he was some kind of official Zionist representative) Mr. Szereszewski was on the most cordial terms with my father, a dedicated Bundist. I asked my father to ask Mr. Szereszewski if there was any way I could use the pool, at least once, and he did so immediately. Mr. Szereszewski said he would be delighted to bring me as a guest, a friend of his family. "And Halina, too?" I mumbled. "Of course, with the greatest of pleasure," replied Mr. Szereszewski.

I immediately ran to Halina to tell her the good news, but she demurred, saying she had no bathing suit. "What does it matter?" I replied expansively, my heart pounding wildly, "Just wear panties. Who cares?" She pondered, then agreed - she agreed, that gorgeous adorable angel of my dreams - she agreed! Her parents and mine suspected nothing. How obtuse these old folks were about the inner lives of their offspring!

And so, half an hour later, we were splashing in the pool, Halinka laughing delightedly, and I - unable to see whether her panties were transparent but satisfying myself that her breasts had (barely) begun to swell - filled with indescribable bliss. We had the pool to ourselves. The middle-aged Humbert Humbert never experienced so delicious a sense of triumph as I did on that brilliant spring morning so long ago. Had I lost my virginity then - a thought that did not enter my head at that time - I could not have been more ecstatic.

The boat sailed on, each day merging into the next, the sea calm, the sun dazzling, the ping-pong balls plink-plinking, the passengers sun-bathing, reading, promenading, conversing, sometimes stopping to argue about something or other, their hands gesticulating, and then resuming their stroll. On May Day the Bundists gathered to sing the Internationale and the Bundist hymn "The Vow" ("We vow our loyalty to the Bund - only it can free the downtrodden slaves"), both, of course, sung in Yiddish. One of the comrades made an appropriate speech. I joined in the singing, as did the other young votaries, and I found myself, as always, choked up with emotion at the words *a shvue, a shvue, on grenetsn dem bund* (a vow, a vow without limits to the Bund). At such solemn moments, no one stopped to ponder how the Bund could ever set itself the task of "freeing the downtrodden slaves," either now or in the future. One does not question sacred rituals.

I have often wondered how many of the Polish-Jewish passengers on that ship knew what was going on in the world at that time, especially in their distant homeland. No one, as far as I remember, had a short wave radio. In Poland the process of mass extermination had not yet been launched, but Nazi intentions and abilities were only too well known. The ghettos in Warsaw, Lodz, and other cities were already in place. The Soviet Union still ruled eastern Poland. Operation Barbarossa was little more than a month away, Pearl Harbor seven months in the future. In Japan we had had access to radios, and the telephone kept us in touch with the Jewish Labor Committee in New York, which sponsored and helped to finance our trip to the United States. Those who knew English could also obtain the press bulletins issued by the US embassy in Tokyo and its consulate in Yokohama. Here in the middle of the Pacific Ocean, what information was available? None, I imagine. How much did my parents and their friends know about the thousands of people already being decimated by typhus and starvation in the ghettos, about the ubiquitous signs that warned Poles not to come near the lice-infested Jews, about the thousands who were being expelled from their homes and towns all over Poland and sent to extermination camps?

Maybe they were glad to have a brief interval free of the most up-to-date news. But with or without it, the adults had boarded the boat carrying a burden of heart-sickening knowledge that could only get heavier. For them there was no escape from their memories, not even in the middle of the Pacific Ocean. For me, despite the difficult and often distressing months under the Soviets and for all the political wisdom I had imbibed in my short life, the journey was part of a grand adventure that tended to displace harrowing thoughts about Poland and those I had left behind. Perhaps it was the triumph of youth over experience...

About ten days after we had sailed from Japan, the *Asama Maru* steamed into the Honolulu for an eighteen-hour stay. I looked, perplexed, at a group of burly men swinging their legs over the boxes they were sitting on, guzzling milk from containers and smoking big fat cigars. Their girth notwithstanding, they decidedly did not resemble "capitalists," the one species I had always associated with cigar smoking. As usual, I turned to my father for an explanation of this extraordinary sight. He replied that in America even workers, including stevedores like these men, smoked cigars.

We disembarked, and boarded a tourist bus that took us to the city and surrounding hills, parks and beaches. For lunch we went to a large restaurant where mumu-clad and lei-garlanded Hawaiian girls performed "authentic" Hawaiian dances. I found it all marvelous, including the huge bowls of mixed fruit, never before part of any normal menu I'd known. My mother, a nurse and somewhat obsessed with nutritional matters (a major item for the children in the Sanatorium), pronounced the food "a most wholesome treat." In the evening we returned to the boat, and the following morning, just before daybreak, the boat resumed its journey. The sun continued to shine, the sea to sparkle, but the games my friends and I played were beginning to wear thin, and I had come to the bottom of my pile of Sherlock Holmes novels. (The ship's library, unsurprisingly, carried no books in either Polish or Yiddish.) I made one more foray into the swimming pool, though unhappily this time without my lovely friend Halina.

Finally, on May 10, 1941, our boat passed under the Golden Gate. It looked breathtaking, as did the port and buildings on the hills above us. With newly-stamped passports we left the customs and immigration offices, and were greeted by several Bundists we did not know personally, but who embraced us with joy, as if we were long-lost relatives. *Mishpokhedikayt* again! Overwhelmed, we loaded ourselves and our luggage into a taxi, and were driven straight to a hotel. Our host, a short man of about fifty, ran ahead, filled out the registration forms, and then took us by lift to the fourth floor. There he again ran ahead, key in hand. After opening the door to our room he led us into the bathroom, where he triumphantly turned the faucet over the sink, saying excitedly, "You see? Running water!" A immigrant who had left a small *shtetl* in Poland twenty or thirty years before, he had no way of knowing that our lower-middle-class apartment in Warsaw boasted hot and cold water, a tub, even a shower. My mother smiled. My father broke into a grin: "America!" he said quietly, his eyes sparkling.

7

Los Angeles 1941-42

The Bund in the New World. A Tempting Offer. So How do You Like this Country? Into Long Pants. Conversing with the Natives. Yiddish Under the Palms. A Personal Holocaust. Back to Los Angeles. Wowing Them.

Most of the Jewish families that arrived from Poland in the United States in 1940-41, either via Yokohama or later via Shanghai, landed in New York, that historic haven for huddled masses, and were then packed off by their host organizations – the Joint Distribution Committee, the Jewish Labor Committee, HIAS, or religious charities – to furnished apartments in the Bronx, Brooklyn, and Manhattan. A few more prosperous families, hardly any Bundists among them, had succeeded in booking seats on the few planes still flying out of beleaguered Warsaw (subject to Luftwaffe attacks from the first day of the war), and, after greasing the palms of successive government officials, had managed to reach Spain or Portugal and thence, eventually, by boat or plane, the United States.

For the Bundists, culture shock was cushioned by the large number of friends or relatives who were there to greet them in the spirit of *mishpokhedikayt*. A year or two earlier, when they left

Warsaw to escape from the advancing German army, they found temporary refuge among Bundist families in the *shtetlekh* and towns along the way. Circumstances were now altogether different, yet the cordiality and concern of the American hosts - most of whom knew the Bundists only by reputation - hardly differed from what the Bundists had experienced back in September 1939.

Indeed, it almost seemed as if the Bund, a party firmly rooted in the "here and now" of Jewish life in Eastern Europe, committed to a version of Marxian socialism and to the strengthening of Yiddish culture, transcended geographic boundaries. The leaders of the Workmen's Circle, largest of all the "fraternal orders" created in the US earlier in the century by Jewish immigrants from Eastern Europe, had almost to a man cut their political teeth in the underground Bund or in other clandestine political parties in Tsarist Russia. The first newspaper the new immigrants laid eyes on was the *forverts*, the largest Yiddish daily, many of whose contributors had once been Bundists or Mensheviks (Russian democratic socialists), such as Rafael Abramovitch and David Shub. (Some of the latter's books, such as his biography of Lenin, first appeared in the pages of the *forverts*.) The head of the large International Ladies Garment Workers Union was David Dubinsky, a baker's apprentice and Bundist activist in Lodz around the turn of the century. Arrested and dispatched to Siberia for his revolutionary activities, Dubinsky managed to escape en route (as did others) and then made his way to the United States. *"ikh bin nokh alts a getrayer bundist"* (I remain to this day a loyal Bundist), he assured his new *khaveyrim*, usually adding , *"nor in Amerike!"* (only in America) . Most Bundists, like my father, prided themselves on the sophistication that they felt distinguished them from their hosts, most of whom had never, during their pre-emigration days, had the experience of working in an open or semi-open political system, and they refused to be swayed by their hosts' ardent, embarrassingly provincial American patriotism. Nevertheless, they too were duly impressed by Dubinsky's Horatio Alger saga. "Think of it," said my father, "a poor half-educated baker from Lodz becoming head of one of the most powerful unions in the United States!" It was enough to shake one's abhorrence of capitalism.

The cachet enjoyed by the newcomers guaranteed not only a friendly reception but also entry into the job market: despite their lack of knowledge of English, many of the new émigrés found employment in labor unions and in Jewish organizations (no dearth of the latter). Some who had worked for years as trade union or party officials or as white collar workers in Poland now rejoined the ranks of the proletariat, becoming "cutters" or "pressers" in the garment industry, working cheek by jowl with Italian, Puerto Rican and American Jewish workers (a majority at that time). These, mostly in their late 30s or early 40s, were sufficiently robust, physically and mentally, to turn over a new page in their lives. My mother, on the other hand, a registered nurse in Poland, refused even to consider "retooling" or taking courses that could lead to a legitimate nursing job in the States. Instead, she proceeded to cultivate would once have been called "neurasthenic" symptoms; the whole family paid a heavy price for my mother's apparently psychosomatic ailments. Mainly, it meant that she would not be considered for a job in her field.

The fortunes of my own small family had much in common with those of other Bundists: we too were warmly welcomed by former members and admirers of the Bund, but unlike the subway-riders and apartment-renters of New York, our Los Angeles hosts were bona fide "alrightniks", their difficult transitions behind them. They owned homes with cactus and flower-lined gardens, and drove automobiles they would trade in after barely one year (with a cash supplement), for the latest models - a feature of American opulence that I found extraordinary.

What persuaded my parents to stay in Los Angeles instead of proceeding to New York, as did almost all of the Bundists? New York was becoming the center of Bundist life in America. My parents' friends, and also most of my coevals, especially those I befriended during our two indolent months in Japan, had gone east immediately. But despite the help of their hosts, in the first place the Jewish Labor Committee (which had helped to finance their odyssey from Poland to the States), my parents worried about the prospects of landing a good job in New York. As for me, my parents reasoned that finding new friends and adjusting to a new milieu would not prove all that traumatic - in fact, it might turn out a salutary experience.

What tipped the scales, however, was an offer that my father found too tempting to ignore: namely, to become the director of the Workmen's Circle Yiddish school in Los Angeles, a job that would also involve some teaching and lecturing to adult audiences in and around Los Angeles. The proposition included a handsome salary.

My parents accepted the offer with alacrity. They realized that the circumstances would be hugely different from those that prevailed in pre-war Poland, where many Jewish schools of every ideological stripe were full day schools, often teaching almost all courses in Yiddish or Hebrew. Here, classes were held only a few afternoons a week, and once during the weekend. Moreover, while many "second generation" children still spoke Yiddish until well into the early 1930s, this was no longer the case. Whenever possible, teachers would speak in Yiddish – but students would almost invariably reply in English.

My father got the offer in May or June; the job would begin the next September. Meanwhile, my own future had to be settled. People with vivid memories of crippling poverty, censorship and pervasive anti-Semitism kept asking me how I liked America, and were at the least taken aback when I responded, rebelliously, that America was not the best thing I'd ever seen! Vexed by their smug if understandable assumptions, I told my concerned well-wishers, with ill-suppressed disdain, of the many things I disapproved of in my new adopted homeland. In fact, I even insisted - with more heat than reason - that I saw our sojourn in the United States as a temporary refuge, and that in a short time we would return to Poland. It was a piece of childish obduracy, and my interlocutors were plainly disconcerted. They glanced at each other in surprise, wondering what could possibly make this apparently good natured and intelligent young man spout such nonsense.

In any case, school would presumably cure me of these perverse notions. My parents found something called the "Foreign Adjustment Section," part of a large junior high school located on a hilltop in the center of town, whose students were drawn exclusively from foreign countries. The person who chauffered us through Los Angeles, a soft-spoken man by the named of Feiner, took us to meet the principal of the school. I was put off by the severe urban architecture of the buildings and grounds: bricks, cement, a wrought iron fence, with not a piece of greenery anywhere, despite Los Angeles' lush foliage! In addition, the din produced by the students on the playground during the frequent recesses was deafening, yet seemed to concern the teachers not at all. Decorum, European-style, was certainly not the name of the game.

Feiner conducted all the negotiations, translating questions and answers for my parents and myself: my mother did not know a word of English, my father only thought he did, and mine, from the English course I took in the Vilna *gimnazye* for three months, was not much better. I was nervous, feeling the eyes of students upon me and hearing giggles and laughter... Soon came the coup de grace: a hefty Mexican lad, perhaps 16 or 17 years old, approached me from behind and delivered a resounding smack on my behind, which delighted the kids looking on and brought tears to my eyes – tears not of pain but of humiliation. I knew the cause of this contemptuous welcome: I was wearing shorts - normal in Europe, a side-splitting sight in the States, where, as I was soon to find out, boys over three wore long pants and girls over two sported skirts or shorts.

With the paper work out of the way, I announced in a tone that brooked no disagreement that I must, right now, and not a minute later, obtain a pair of long pants. Mr. Feiner obliged and soon we found ourselves in a Jewish haberdashery store where I was outfitted with a splendid pair of dark light-weight trousers. Now I could fearlessly face the future.

Well, not quite. The first few days in my new surroundings I found myself at sixes and sevens, either accompanying my parents in their search for a suitable apartment, or pacing the grubby streets of Boyle Heights and listening to the mutilated Yiddish of our Americanized neighbors. The bizarre formulations of "Yinglish" provided me and my parents with endless hours of mirth, and solidified my disdain for the cultural primitivism of the American Jew.

Two incidents in particular come to mind. Once, on a visit to our new acquaintances, the lady of the house, intent on making me feel more secure, thrust a quarter into my hand, and suggested that I walk down the street to the nearest bakery. "Just say 'please give me a loaf of rye bread'," said the lady pleasantly. "Or come to think of it," she added, brightening up, "you can say it in Yiddish, too: *git mir a rye bred, pleez.* I am sure you will manage!" *Mirabile dictu,* I did.

The second incident concerned my mother. We spent the first few days in L.A. in a small two-story hotel in Boyle Heights. My mother, intrigued by the huge consumption of cold milk by young and old, bought herself a bottle of milk in a local grocery. But how to keep it cool? There certainly was no refrigerator in our hotel room. A concerned neighbor - perhaps the same accommodating lady who sent me out for a loaf of rye - suggested that she place the bottle *"oyf der vinde." "Vinde?"* my mother was nonplussed. This was the word used in Yiddish for "elevator," from the Polish word *"winda."* How, she wondered, could a bottle of milk keep cool and not churn into butter as it rode up and down in the elevator? The mystery was soon cleared up: *"Vinde"* was our neighbor's "Yinglish" for "window." Enlightened, my mother deferred her next milk purchase until we were safely ensconced in our new apartment, fully furnished, including a snappy frigidaire. One of four family units in a small house, it was a few blocks from DeSoto Boulevard, the main drag of Boyle Heights. (I had my first American haircut on that busy road: normally it cost 50 cents, but the barber had a Jewish heart, and knocked off a dime for the new kid.)

Directly below us lived a pudgy little man, a former Bundist trade union official, his anxious, bustling wife and a daughter approximately my age (equipped, I did not fail to notice, with firm breasts even an older girl might take pride in). Whatever my fantasies, they gradually broke down in a messy attempt to unsnap a recalcitrant bra that would not detach itself from her slippery shoulders: we were both extraordinarily clumsy when it came to the most elementary steps of "kissing" and "petting," the distinctions between these two eluding me for some time. With some relief we gave up our fumbling to return to a comfortable relationship consisting of long discussions (in Polish; Irene hardly knew any Yiddish) about books, films, and common friends. Not for us, young European intellectuals, the graceless joys of experimental coupling.

And so the desultory summer days and evenings dragged on, punctuated occasionally by a visit to a local swimming pool, where

Los Angeles: 1941-1942   65

I felt more isolated among crowds of teen-agers than during my solitary walks on the city streets, or by trips to a local cinema or visits with my parents to one of their hospitable new friends, where I usually avoided getting tipsy on either of the two wines proffered by our host, "sour" (white) or "sweet" (red, invariably my preference). As for the youngsters of my own age, I envied their apparent confidence, their easy-going manners, so at odds with my own self-conscious behavior. Envy, unless confronted honestly, tends to degenerate into surliness and anger, even into smoldering contempt for the putative culprits.

The situation in school was no better. I took typing, which proved very useful, but courses in English and literature, not to mention arithmetic, were a pain. At regular "assembly hours" we were all taught to sing Stephen Foster songs, and a rousing – and obligatory – number called "I am an American of the USA." The diverse Chinese, Mexican, Italian, Japanese and German accents delivering one proto-lingual hymn may have amused the teachers, but did little to teach the students to distinguish between "I am an Amelican of da USA" and "Mine hart trobs meet confidence facing each new day" and on to "zees rivers, zees fields are mine all mine!" Still, it was all buoyant and merry, even if it did not teach us to distinguish sibilants from palatals, or dentals from fricatives. Only a course in remedial English several years later helped to set me straight on such essential matters.

At the end of that mercifully brief stay at Central Junior High School I was sent by my parents to a hilly and dusty region near San Diego which housed the Workmen's Circle summer camp, a rough-and-tumble collection of frame houses and tents, as well as a swimming pool - the main venue for sexually aroused teen-age males to ogle thinly-clad pubescent female bodies and vice versa. I had never seen so much young uninhibited sexuality on display; all it did was intensify my loneliness and melancholy. I just could not, could not be a carefree American of the USA! Personal history, layers of anxieties, suspicion, articulated and inarticulated resentments all combined to make me aggressive, testy, and sullen.

At the same time, the camp authorities took pride in affirming a loyalty to High Culture: every afternoon the campers would lie around outside listening to orchestral music blazing from a public address system, the favorite being Beethoven's Fifth Symphony with its stuttering opening themes. It was somehow not entirely real, but it did endow life in the camp with a Higher Purpose. As the majestic music rose through the air, the usually boisterous and garrulous youngsters fell silent and then, when it was over, stood up, still silent, as if mesmerized, and entered the dining room. Within two minutes, the ruckus was back full-force.

In September 1941 I entered Hollenbeck Junior High School, a far more meritorious institution than the one I had attended after our arrival. As a reward for my cooperation, I was assigned to the fiddle-section of the high school orchestra, bravely scratching out the theme of Haydn's Surprise Symphony. It was certainly better than bellowing "I am an American of the USA..." However, I had to recognize that the process of becoming integrated into the mainstream of American life was going to be arduous. Hence, I opted enthusiastically for an area of endeavor which I could certainly stake out for myself, and which offered me a chance of self-fulfillment. I am speaking of Yiddish.

The Los Angeles Jewish community boasted its own small intellectual elite that cushioned my parents' entry into a world at once familiar and bizarre. They were mostly unemployed journalists, free-lance writers, and retired actors, who had left the bleak tenement houses in the Bronx and Brooklyn in search of the sun and languorous climate that Southern California offered in such abundance. For a Yiddish intelligent to move from New York to Los Angeles meant to distance him- or herself from the turbulent and exhilarating center of Yiddish literary life, with its daily newspapers (four of them in the early 1940s), publishing houses, journals, Maurice Schwartz's Yiddish Art Theater on Second Avenue and the itinerant theatrical groups almost always hawking their fare (of various degrees of mediocrity). It meant no longer looking frantically for an empty chair in one of the cafes where you could eavesdrop on the latest literary and personal gossip for and it meant you could no longer attend public lectures by the occasional celebrity from Poland, Romania, or Argentina.

But Los Angeles offered certain compensations to the Yiddish-speaking intelligent. The *forverts* printed a special West Coast edition published in L.A.; writers and artists would visit to lecture and perform. Nor was the local literary colony composed exclusively of second stringers or men and women worn out by the madding pace of New York. Two men in particular lent it at least a patina of sophistication. One was the gifted playwright Peretz Hirzhbeyn, author of *grine felder* and *di puste kretchme* (Green Fields; The Haunted Inn), the other a fine actor from the famous if defunct theatrical group The Vilna Troupe, Noyakh Nakhbush. The LA intellectuals did not regard them as legitimate *toyshvim* (natives) – to join the ranks of the *toyshvim*, you had to have settled in L.A. by the early 1930s – but rather as welcome guests who would readily leave for other pastures at a moment's notice.

They were not altogether wrong. Nakhbush, after a spell in L.A., proceeded to New York and was soon forgotten there, a man who could not find himself a niche in a city dominated artistically by Maurice Schwartz and, alas, by various degrees of *shund* (literary trash). As for Hirzhbeyn, a man of inexhaustible energy even in his sixties, a world traveler, playwright, producer and theater director, he might have come to Los Angeles in 1940 expecting to move on to some other town or country, but he apparently succumbed to the allurements of the city, and felt less inclined to resume his peripatetic way of life. He died in 1949. In my memory Hirzhbeyn was a lanky man, with a crop of light hair falling over his forehead, a melancholy mien and a feeble voice one had to strain to hear. I remember him standing before an audience, entwining his fingers and saying tremulously: "Yes, my friends, there are only two things in this world - honor and honorarium" (*yo, mayne fraynd, es zenen do nor tsvey zakhn in der velt – honor un honorar*). The audience loved it.

But whatever pride the Yiddish intelligentsia took in Hirzhbeyn and Nakhbush, their real enthusiasm was focused on the poet Malke Heifetz Tuzman (Tussman), admittedly a minor talent, but a *toyshev* like themselves. She was an attractive woman in her early forties, with dark hair and what would have been called in the 1970s an earth-mother smile; she wore a long skirt and a long fringed shawl. Shortly after our arrival in Los Angeles, she invited my family and a few friends for a picnic to one of the city's handsome parks. I still have a photograph of that event: my father, his tie undone, his jacket lying near-by, reclining on a pile of leaves, smiling happily into the camera, my mother in a large hat, sitting primly to his right, myself to his left, in a pose identical to my father's, also smiling into the camera, and six other local friends, all obviously enjoying the occasion.

Malke Tuzman was not an outstanding poet, and her verse seldom made it into the chrestomaties published in New York, but occasional pieces of hers, lyrical, quiet and feminist and mildly erotic, were published in literary journals such as *tsukunft* and others. In an age of true literary giants such as H. Leivick, M.L. Halperin, Jacob Gladshteyn, Avrom Sutskever and Itzik Manger she could not aspire to prominence - except, that is, in California, where she was unquestioningly A Major and Most Beloved Yiddish Poet. Several decades later, with almost all of the Yiddish writers already gone, she became the object of a minor cult by young students of Yiddish poetry, who published and analyzed her works, and taped, as I recall, one video interview with her. She died in 1971.

We also had a truly minor Yiddish poet in Los Angeles, a neighbor of ours in Boyle Heights, whose surname was Gold but whose first name I cannot recall nor find in any anthologies. Unlike Tuzman, Gold wrote prolifically, but had no luck when he sent his work off for consideration. He was forced to scrape together some of his own savings plus a few donations from friends, to produce a volume. Once published, he would declaim his verse at dinner parties and, with an insistence that would have been more profitably expended on other endeavors, at the literary gatherings to which he was infrequently invited.

The trouble with Gold – a big man and quite excitable - was not only the absolute mediocrity of his poetry. He was also a Communist, naïve beyond belief, to whom every bit of Soviet casuistry, however inane, was Holy Writ. My father, by temperament not confrontational, would grimace uncomfortably at the very mention of Gold's name. He groaned whenever Gold turned up, bursting with anticipation for another political-literary dispute with my father on such issues as the artistic freedom available to writers in the Soviet Union, from which he would invariably emerge the loser, yet cheerful and amicable all the same. After thanking my father for a "most enlightening chat," he would take his leave, after which my father would utter a sigh of relief and exclaim, to no one in particular, "*saran onshikenish!*" (what a nuisance or plague). Had Gold been a knowledgeable and intelligent adversary, my father would not have minded the occasional contretemps. But Gold was a card-carrying *yold* (fool) and a *nudnik*, the kind of person whose very appearance makes you want to cross the street hurriedly in order to avoid him.

Eventually, perhaps finally sensing my father's impatience, Gold decided to make me the subject of his proselytizing zeal, but he struck out once more. I had experienced enough Soviet reality and, from my father and other Bundists, imbibed so many anti-communist arguments that I had no compunctions, young and brash as I was, about using them on our local True Believer, and I remember with amusement our occasional battles. I remain grateful to Gold, however, for teaching me several Yiddish songs - all, naturally, of Soviet provenance, but like so many Soviet songs, with superb melodies. One in particular stayed with me during all these years. Translated from Belorussian, it depicts (oh Brave New World!) the visit of one group of collective farmers to another, and with all its anodyne agitprop lyrics I still find it charming:

iz zayts mikh un hots mikh un lebt in ashires
un mir veln forn tsurik in di dires.
mir hobn gehuliet mit ale tsuzamen,
s'hot keyner gezen nokh a yontev aza min.
Fare you well, dear comrades, and continue to prosper,
While we must head back to our homes and our pastures.
We sang and were merry till the dawn's early hours,
There was never a fete quite as joyful as ours!

If Gold's politics irritated my father, it was because he nursed a particular enmity for zealous Communist apologists in general. The small Lithuanian-Polish *shtetl* of Swieciany, with a fairly large Jewish population, including several members of my father's family, had in the course of 1917 and 1918 been invaded, by the Whites, by the Red Army, by Ukrainian bands. On one such "visit", the Bolsheviks seized ten distinguished citizens to be executed for the help the town had ostensibly given to the White Guardists, who only two days earlier had abandoned Swieciany after a three-week occupation. The victims were lined up against a wall and killed in a single burst of machine-gun fire. Among them were my father's father - my grandfather - and one of his brothers, my uncle.

I was unaware of this double murder in my father's family until 1965, right after my father's death, when his sister Dora, herself a survivor of a Nazi camp, told me this story. "I don't know how I can go on," she said, now that she outlived her last sibling. She did, of course, clinging to life for the same reason she had done so back in the German camp - to help her daughter Sara, then aged 10, to survive. At one desperate point she suggested to Sara that they swallow the two pills of cyanide she had carried around with her since their arrest. But Sara would have none of it. "I want to live!" she exclaimed, weeping uncontrollably, with a force her mother would never have expected of her mild daughter. Dora died perhaps twenty years after my father, with Sara by her bedside. Sara herself, my only surviving cousin, died after a long bout with cancer, surrounded by husband and offspring, just a few weeks before I sat down to pen these lines.

My father's family thus experienced its own holocaust: my grandfather and one uncle killed by the Bolsheviks in 1918; an aunt, Maryla, who in 1938 went to Minsk to marry a man she fell in love with during her earlier visit to the Soviet Union, and perished in the ghetto; another brother of my father, the youngest in the family, Berek, exiled by the Soviets in 1939. He married a Russian woman and began raising a family. Until 1943 we would get letters from him, once including a photograph of himself and his wife. In 1943 they disappeared without a trace. In 1999, I visited Swieciany for the first time since 1938. A woman in the town who had known my relatives, including my grandmother, told me of the destruction of the Swieciany ghetto. I went to the local cemetery and saw gravestones inscribed with the family name Brumberg - a fair number of them. Of my mother's relatives in Warsaw, only one, a brother, survived. The rest - mother, sister, brother-in-law and two children, cousins - died either in the conflagration in Warsaw or in Treblinka.

In Los Angeles my father's hosts and benefactors explained to him that before he assumed his new duties as a director cum teacher, he had plenty of time to perform his other function - namely, as a lecturer.

My father took this in stride, for as a Bundist leader in Poland he would often travel from one end of the country to another to lecture on topics from "The world of Sholem Aleichem" to "The Future of Socialism." Much the same was expected of him in California. One thing that he did not expect were the flowery tributes that preceded his lecture: those who introduced him attributed to him feats of intellectual and political achievements to which he could under no circumstances aspire, but which in the circumstances he could hardly deny without making them – or himself - look foolish. Once, back from one of his trips, my father regaled my mother and myself with stories of how he was introduced as "one of the most celebrated leaders of the Bund," or "that famous writer and thinker," or "the man we have all been waiting to hear," or no less than "the Sun of Europe!" Such verbal extravagance was obviously something distinctly American: in Europe it would have provoked considerable embarrassment.

One day, while preparing himself for a lecture on the Yiddish poet Abraham Liesin, a man more celebrated for his ringing nationalist and socialist verse than for his prosodic talents, my father asked me whether I might not like to accompany him and declaim some of Liesin's poetry. I accepted his suggestion with alacrity, and soon found myself in front of an auditorium of perhaps a hundred people reciting some of Liesin's hortatory verse, possibly from Liesin's 1911 ode *tsum ershtn may* (to May Day):

fun di lender fun di vayte, durkh di yamen durkh di breyte,
kumt der liber friling vint in di shtet in di farshtikte, tsvishn moy-
ern ayngedrikte
tsum farshmakhtn mentshns–kind.
oyf bashtralte fliglen shvebt er, un a shtraln shire tsilt er
in di hertser mild arayn, un di mentshn tif-baglikte, oyfge-
munterte, antsikte
zapn ayn dos likht fun shayn.

From far off lands and spacious oceans comes the lovely wind of spring,
Through suffocating cities and walls pressed together
It reaches the languishing son of man.

It hovers on radiant wings, a song of rays gently piercing
the hearts of people
Who, drunk with happiness, cheered and rapturous
Imbibe the song of light.

I might have recited one of Liesin's much simpler paeans to future bliss:

es vet kumen di tsayt un di tsayt iz nit vayt,
un fun mayrev, fun mizrakh, fun yetvider zayt, ariber der elnder velt
vet derheybn zikh shturmik a glutiker vint
un es veln di volkns farshvindn geshvind
fun blayenem himl-getselt
Oh, the time it will come very soon, very soon,
From the West, from the East and from everywhere all over
the lonely world,
A tempestuous wind will erupt and dispel
The clouds that are hanging above.

Now, nearly a century after they were penned, and six decades after I declaimed them, these verses elicit an acute sense of embarrassment. The early "proletarian poets," such as Morris Vinchevsky and Morris Rosenfeld, not to speak of the guileless and enchanting Avrom Reizen, were by comparison with Liesin masterful craftsmen, perhaps poor in their poetic lexicon yet capable of writing verse that arose from the depths of Jewish experience and touched the hearts of their readers. They went on to develop their skills and expand the limits of poetic expression. Liesin, however, remained mired in the same *trafaretn* (clichés), the same clumsy, uninspired language and imagery with which he started in Minsk at the turn of the century and to which he stuck resolutely until his death in 1938.

Why, then, did my father, himself a lover of Pushkin and Lermontov, have to discourse on the merits of such a rhymester as Liesin? I do not know for certain, but unlike Vinchevsky and others, Liesin came to dominate the literary landscape of the United States, and also to assume important positions, such as the editorship of the best literary journal, *di tsukunft*, which kept him for a long time in the public eye. Furthermore, Liesin was not a sectarian: he embraced socialism and Zionism and Yiddishism with equal zeal, and thus did not become embroiled in factional struggles that characterized Jewish secular life in the first part of the 20th century. And so he became, in the eyes of his constituents, the troubadour of all the major creeds of modern Jewishness. How could one be against Liesin?

At any rate, the evening – including my recitation - was a success, and led to more performances, so much so that in time I became known in Yiddish circles as no less than *"Avremele dos vunderkind fun poyln"* (Avremele, the prodigal from Poland). My parents disapproved; I enjoyed my small fame. In fact, things got more complex, inasmuch as Nakhbush, tired of his exclusively one-man performances and not finding a single person to join him on the stage, invited me to join him a few times at the Workmen's Circle Center. I was thrilled to appear on stage together with the almost legendary Noyakh Nakhbush! The repertoire chosen by Nakhbush was rather flimsy: two one-act, two-character comedies by Sholem Aleichem, not among the bard's most memorable works, but sidesplitting nevertheless. The mise-en-scène was appropriately modest: a few chairs, a table, a lamp, and a curtain of two sheets stitched together: some sort of a curtain, Nakhbush insisted, was *de rigueur*.

In time, these thespian experiences began to go to my head, and I began fantasizing a theatrical career on the Yiddish stage. This was a bizarre notion. The fact that in 1941-42 Noyakh Nakhbush could not find a single youngster but myself to whom he could teach a few lines of a simple Sholem Aleichem farce was a somber portent of things to come. Ironically, at what seemed to many people, especially those madly enamored of Yiddish, its very effervescent height, Yiddish poetry and prose had embarked on its final decline. The decline later came to be seen as a consequence of the Holocaust in Europe, Soviet extinction of Yiddish culture and anti-Semitism, as well as the ruthless *Kulturkampf* waged by mainstream Israeli Zionists against the "rotten culture of the Diaspora" - that is, Yiddish.

But at the time, Panglossian optimism prevailed. The Los Angeles Yiddish *forverts* began printing announcements featuring my name right next to my father's or Noakh Nakhbush's, as well as stories about forthcoming lectures, recitals and plays. One such story, perhaps the most imaginative of all, I still recall: "'Yes!' say the Jews of Los Angeles, 'a concert such as the one we shall hear this coming Sunday at 5 pm at the Workmen's Circle House, featuring the learned Joseph Brumberg and his son Avremele the Prodigal from Poland, we shall never, ever forget'."

And so, for a few months, Yiddish life in Los Angeles was treated to a shot in the arm, with "the sun of Europe" lecturing in Yiddish-speaking communities, his gifted son reciting Yiddish poetry, and Noyakh Nakhbush providing a bit of theatrical lore along with his sidekick Avremele. Not for long, however. By the autumn of 1941 I was already a student in a normal junior high school in Boyle Heights, able to imbibe the native Boyle Heights accent, like all the youngsters around me. Unable to mix with my coevals in Yiddish, I became gradually alienated from the new culture, and developed an increasing resentment for Los Angeles, its denizens, and everything that its culture presumably stood for. Needless to say, this was far more a reflection of my values and anxieties than of the real state of things.

As the school year passed, my father was losing his taste for teaching boys and girls with only a smattering of Yiddish, and for roaming about Southern California delivering lectures on Yiddish literature, fascism, and the ever-receding vision of socialism, whose bright light seemed to be flickering. After Pearl Harbor, the much touted tolerance and generosity of the American people turned into sour, snide and vulgar jingoism, and wholesale unsubstantiated charges against Japanese-Americans - the new "fifth column" - filled the air. Then came the massive deportations of Japanese-Americans from the West coast into hurriedly constructed barracks forming large concentration camps, something I became eerily aware of when traveling by streetcar through the one-time noisy and colorful Japanese quarter: stores and windows were boarded up, policemen patrolled the streets amid an atmosphere of dread and suspicion.

The news from Poland grew more macabre. No one knew exactly what was happening to the three and a half million Jewish hostages left in Nazi hands and my parents, like myself, felt more acutely the need to be among our own people, that is to say the by now large Bundist colony in New York City. Thus soon thereafter my father served notice that he was withdrawing from his public lectures and thus my public recitations, too, and that he would leave by the end of the academic year 1941-1942. The Los Angeles *toyshvim*, who had become fond of my parents, were sorry to see us go, but they understood the reasons. As for myself, I could hardly contain my delight at the prospect of being reunited with my old friends.

In the summer of 1942, we boarded a train for New York. In Los Angeles, a new teacher was found to take my father's place. But the excitement generated by my father's presence was gone. And shortly thereafter the Los Angeles edition of the *forverts* went out of business.

8

Tumultuous Teens

The Bronx. Avrom Reizin. A European Amongst Americans. A Communist Teacher. Rebel with Causes. The Two Brothers Weinreich. Honor The Memory. Life Goes On...

My parents and I arrived in New York City in early August 1943, and immediately moved into a small apartment near Van Cortland Park, in the Bronx, courtesy of the Jewish Labor Committee, our patrons and sponsors since early 1940. Established in 1934 in New York by several trade union organizations and the Workmen's Circle, the largest Jewish secular federation, the JLC's main purpose was to help labor leaders and socialists persecuted by the Nazis (and then by the Soviet Union) to survive financially and obtain visas to the United States: it was the JLC that helped us and other Bundists in Soviet-occupied Lithuania succeed in obtaining visas for Japan and thence for the United States.

Now, two years on, the JLC came again to the aid of their European comrades by furnishing them with accommodation and, whenever necessary, with some funds to tide them over until they found work (which most of them did) and could resume a more normal existence.

Our apartment, on the fourth floor of a six-story building at the end of a block, consisted of two rooms, a bathroom, and a tiny kitchen, just large enough for the three of us to have our meals at the table. My mother could dish out the food without having to stand up, since the oven was only inches away from her chair. One of the two rooms became mine, and the other (sometimes doubling as a dining room when guests would come) had a bed that would slide out of a closet, thus turning the room into a bedroom for my parents.

All the windows looked out on an empty lot and beyond that an equally empty street that led to Van Cortland Park, a feast for one's eyes, verdant in the spring and summer, covered with snow in the winter. The house had an elevator. From the sixth floor you clambered up to the roof, which connected to the roof of the neighboring house, a novel but enjoyable way to gain access to the next building.

There, on the fifth floor in a diminutive apartment much like ours, lived a recently arrived Bundist family: the father, an elderly man with no discernible profession either back in Poland or in the United States; the mother, who had been the principal of the second Yiddish school I attended in Warsaw; two daughters, one my age, the other two years older. Neither of them was a raving beauty but both were pleasant looking and had prominent breasts, worthy of my attention. Perhaps having been brought up in accord with some ultra-progressive educational principles, the two sisters were in the habit of walking around in their apartment stark naked, donning some garment or other when somebody was at the door. I discovered that the small peep-hole on the door was uniquely equipped: instead of looking from the inside of the apartment out into the corridor, you could look into the apartment from the outside, and so before ringing the door bell I would spend a few minutes ogling the sisters and getting pleasantly agitated in the process. Occasionally the door was unlocked and I would walk into the apartment with the girls still nude, which seemed not to bother either the parents or the daughters, who would casually proceed to get dressed while I pretended to look the other way. Ah, the charms and frustrations of teenage sex! To my knowledge, none of my other friends or their Bundist parents had the habit of shedding their garments at home, so I doubt whether the family's proclivities had any ideological provenance.

Van Cortland Park offered a host of trails, a lake where you could swim in the summer and ice skate in the winter, and an abundance of grassland, flowers and trees extending for miles. Our small group – mostly children of Bundists, ages eleven to fifteen, joined by two brothers who became my close friends - would go on long hikes, taking along large sandwiches filled with ham and Swiss cheese (neither we nor our parents as yet knew of the fabulous delicatessens that New York was justly famous for). School was still far away, summer seemed endless and our Wanderlust, instilled by the Bundist children organization SKIF to which we had belonged in Poland, seemed unquenchable.

Across the street from our building was a junior high school, and abutting Gouverneur Avenue, one of the main drags of the West Bronx, Sedgwick Avenue. Sedgwick Avenue bordered on a large water reservoir, along which I would walk for the next three years to my high school, DeWitt Clinton. Next to the reservoir there was a small playground where mothers would bring their toddlers to play in the sand or climb the jungle-gym while the ladies would swap the latest gossip.

On the other side of Sedgwick Avenue, facing the reservoir, stood a housing project named after the Amalgamated Clothing Workers' Union, which had built and owned the project for many years. Many of its sunny and spacious flats now housed Bundist immigrants. If you walked on Sedgwick Avenue in the opposite direction you soon came to another housing project, a cooperative called "the Sholem Aleichem Buildings," after the famous Yiddish writer. Many of its residents were teachers, journalists and printers working for one or another of the four Yiddish dailies that came out in New York at that time, all long gone; a weekly edition of the *forverts* still comes out in Yiddish, and an English edition as well.

The most celebrated resident of the Sholem Aleichem Buildings was the aging Yiddish poet Avrom Reizen, a legendary figure for my friends and myself - for hadn't we declaimed and sung his verses in the Yiddish elementary schools in Warsaw and Vilna? A year after arriving in New York, I gathered the courage to ring his doorbell. A slightly stooped figure with gray hair opened the door, obviously quite taken aback by my presence: Reizen would often be invited to Yiddish schools for celebrations in his honor, but clearly it had been a long time since anyone under forty appeared at his doorstep.

He graciously admitted me and led me into his book-lined study, all the time peppering me with questions about myself, my parents and the source of my fluent Yiddish, already a rarity among American Jewish youngsters. Then he took a book off the shelves, saying he would now read to me lines from "the greatest poet who ever lived." This turned out to be Heinrich Heine, whose poems he read to me in German. I hardly understood a word, but felt terribly excited that Reizen would treat me so respectfully, while also marveling that he would so adore a German poet. (In fact in this Reizen was not alone: most Yiddish poets and writers of the last century were admirers of German and Russian 19th century writers.)

In recent years I have occasionally come back to this corner of the world, and found it (not surprisingly) changed almost beyond recognition. The apartment houses, the junior high school, the water reservoir are all still there, unchanged. But Gouverneur Avenue is now lined with high-rise apartment buildings, highways crisscross Van Cortland Park, and I see no one hiking along the trails we so loved. The old pharmacy on Sedgwick Avenue has been transformed into a glittering all-purpose drug store. You hardly hear any Yiddish on the street, but Spanish is ubiquitous, and what used to be the old Jewish ("slice me a rye") bakery, redolent of freshly baked rolls, now purveys empanadas and the like; its bagels, I noticed last time I was there, were delivered by truck from a central bakery somewhere in Queens. Most shocking of all, a bakery that at one time produced as many as six varieties of rolls, now displayed packaged sliced bread on its shelves.

In September 1942 I enrolled at the DeWitt Clinton High School on Sedgwick Avenue, at that time an all-boys school known for its high academic standards. The year I enrolled, there was still a "Classic Languages Department" on the ground floor, though courses in ancient Greek, I was told, had long ago been discontinued and the only course taught by the department was Beginners' Latin. A year later, this, too, was no more. The student body was less than half Jewish, with a variety of other ethnic groups (Irish, Greek, Chinese) in fair abundance, and a small coterie of black students that kept to itself. (I never detected as much as a whiff of racial prejudice at DWC, though I may have been unaware of it; in any event tribalism needs no discrimination to persevere.)

After several weeks of walking by myself to school, which took about fifteen minutes, I found a kindred soul, Abe Goodman, who lived on Sedgwick Avenue and whom I joined on our daily walks to and from DWC. Abe was a quiet boy who read Freud (thus awaking in me a desire to do the same), adored Gilbert and Sullivan operettas and was determined to become a public school teacher when he grew up. (Several years later we met, he a high school teacher and I still in graduate school, and found we no longer had much in common. I think he no longer read Freud any more, either...)

Occasionally I would also walk with a tall boy named Robert Fischer, a Catholic, slightly effeminate, and mad about opera. I once visited him in the miniscule apartment he shared with his mother (his father had left years earlier) where he played some of his favorite records by Puccini, Verdi and Massenet. They were all full-throated tenor arias, and much as I tried, I couldn't muster much enthusiasm for them. Robert in turn was disappointed, and as I recall, after this attempt to infect me with his enthusiasm, gave up and we hardly saw one another again.

Boys who read Freud at the tender age of 15 and cared passionately about Gilbert and Sullivan or Verdi were not the norm in most New York high schools, even at Clinton, though less of a rarity there. Still, I had not established close relations with my schoolmates, or for that matter with any coevals outside high school. With some outstanding exceptions in my honor classes, I regarded most American youngsters with condescension, as undereducated, rude and appallingly uninformed about the world outside the U.S.

I continued, then, like so many of my immigrant friends, to play the role of the "educated" European looking down upon the crass and vulgar Americans, emulating if not quite consciously older West European intellectuals unshakably certain of their cultural superiority. Youngsters of my age were hardly in the same league with bona fide British or French intellectuals and our condescending behavior no doubt was resented or ridiculed by many. But something did separate us from Americans. We did all, as a group, come from intelligentsia families and in addition we had all received a tough political education, which by itself tended to created an uneasy barrier between us and American teenagers.

This is not to say that we were indiscriminately scornful of those around us. I remember several boys at Clinton who positively awed me with their intellect, articulateness and what seemed invincible self-assurance. I envied them, as a working class boy might envy a scion of an aristocratic family, and often speculated about the heights they might scale in the future. Indeed, these days, when I happen to glance at the names listed in my high school yearbook, I wonder what has happened to some of those bright, gifted, articulate boys – though after so long, I am not entirely sure I want to know. Yet even these intelligent and impressive boys still seemed to lack some quality that would make them altogether acceptable to us. Whether it was our political background or the impact of the war years, we felt, at least, wiser and more mature than our classmates. This would occur most often when our discussions touched on the Soviet Union, a subject that would eventually come to dominate my life. Soviet reality, to which we had all become exposed for more than a year, imbued us with a rough sophistication which none of our friends could match.

And not only our friends. There was a teacher in DWC, by the name of Stone, a large hulking man with a crew cut, probably in his early fifties, whose English classes mostly turned into vigorous discussions about American politics and current events. Stone came from Arkansas, where he said he had never seen a live Jew, and had imagined them as two-horned creatures. And so he was pleasantly surprised to find out that Jews looked and acted like most people he knew, and we in turn were pleased to find a man who so gracefully confessed to having at one time harbored, as he put it, "ancient and ridiculous" prejudices.

But there was one area where Mr. Stone would not compromise: the Soviet Union. He was an ardent reader of the fellow-traveling newspaper *PM*, and he and I would get involved in lengthy arguments. It was a curious duel, between a thoroughly American middle-aged man on one side and an adolescent only recently arrived from Eastern Europe on the other. Stone invariably remained courteous and calm, while I was given to emotional crescendos. I am sure that had I succeeded in convincing him that he was wrong, he would have admitted it instantly. I loved him for his honesty and directness, while some of his political notions drove me to despair.

In late 1943-early 1944 a frequent topic was the lack of a " second front," a staple of Soviet propaganda, which charged the Western powers with deliberately putting off the opening of a second front in France so as to gradually sap Russia's strength. Though in his youth Stone knew probably even fewer Communists than Jews, he was firmly convinced that the charges against the Allied powers were correct and that the Soviet Union was a splendid, much-maligned country gallantly bearing the heaviest burden of the war effort. His innocence was as appalling as it was attractive. I wonder what Graham Greene would have made of him.

The air of superiority I affected vis-à-vis Americans, children and adults alike, drove me to flaunt my emotional bonds with Poland and Polish culture. Poland might have been backward in many respects, many of its citizens rabidly anti-Semitic (a prejudice which would, I fervently believed, disappear with the advent of socialism), but it had a magnificent history and an admirable culture and literature. America, I said to myself, was by comparison primitive, its culture materialistic, and its facile assumption of the superiority of things American only evidence of abysmal ignorance. For what did these school mates of mine know about Europe? All that I heard from them was that (an undifferentiated) Europe was dreadfully poor, its workers forced to beg in order to get a square meal, its leaders hopelessly addicted to waging war upon each other.

Furious, I would vent my contempt on my interlocutors, especially those of my own age, by producing chapter and verse ostensibly proving them wrong. Which of course led only to hostility and charges that I myself was absurdly uninformed about the United States. They were no doubt correct, but in my self-righteousness I would passionately reject such allegations.

At bottom, what motivated my rebelliousness and that of many European friends was anger at having been uprooted from our familiar milieu and transported to a country so unlike what we knew and felt at home with. The war had dictated the Vilna interlude. In Japan (even in Moscow) we were tourists. But here in the United States, we were supposed to make peace with the idea of a new homeland. For two years after our arrival, I still nurtured the curious dream of returning to Poland. By 1943-44 information from Poland about the fate of its Jews turned that hope into a nightmare, but that merely foreclosed an option, it hardly assuaged our anger. Nor did we receive gratefully the kindly words of our parents' American friends, who would pat our heads and tell us we should consider ourselves lucky to be in "the most wonderful country in the world." And so we - at any rate, I - continued to reject a world to which, imperceptibly, we were getting gradually adjusted, even - horror upon horror - to be growing fond of.

My rebellion took many forms. For one, I refused to read English books, except those required in my courses. It was an absurd decision, and probably slowed my "Americanization process", but in the end in fact contributed to the expansion of knowledge and education that I have never had cause to regret. Already before the war I was reading Dickens, Jack London, Kipling and Mark Twain in Polish or Yiddish and one or two books by Polish writers. Now I chose exclusively the latter, and read works by good writers such as Henryk Sienkiewicz, Stefan Żeromski, Bolesław Prus and others, whom otherwise I would probably have ignored.

To satisfy my craving for Polish books, I would once a week board an IRT train at Jerome Avenue and 238th Street for an hour-long journey to lower Manhattan (all for a nickel!). The station where I boarded the train was the terminus of that line, and so the cars were relatively clean and never crowded. Within fifteen minutes, however, they would fill up with large numbers of often rank humanity, pushing and shoving their way into the cars. Nobody minded: it was par for the course. When I got off, I walked to a large building at the corner of 10th St and Avenue A, a heavily Polish and Ukrainian area, which housed a branch of the New York Public Branch Library known for its large collection of books in Slavic languages. I would come home exhausted, but proudly clutching to my chest three or four Polish volumes.

Less high-mindedly, I listened every Sunday to a radio program in Polish, called *Polskie Dzwony Jachimowicza* (Jachimowicz's Polish Bells). In addition to mercilessly long commercials advertising pork products, various types of vodka, book shops, amusement centers, and a Polish cemetery, the program consisted of selections by Chopin, Polish folksongs, and *szlagiery* (hit songs), one of which, "*Umówixem się znią na dziewątą*" ("I Made a Date with Her for Nine O'clock") I fancy to this day. (Viewers of Roman Polanski's 2002 film *The Pianist* may recall its hero, Szpilman, sitting in a ghetto café in Warsaw playing a *szlagier*. It happens to be "I Made a Date...," perhaps the most popular song in Warsaw at that time.)

My private rebellion lasted over a year. I ingested a good share of modern Polish literature and enlarged my Polish vocabulary, which before the war was far from fluent, since I used it much less than I did Yiddish. Eventually I began to read American literature, especially Sinclair Lewis, whose astringent view of the United States appealed to me no end. Of other books that I favored at that time I remember Kipling's *The Light that Failed*, and the marvelous science fiction adventures by Jules Verne, some of which I had read in Yiddish in Vilna two or three years earlier.

I was also succumbing slowly to the allure of New York, occasionally venturing, with a friend or two, into Chinatown, or "Little Italy" or Central Park, or along luxurious Fifth Avenue with its beautiful window displays and smartly dressed men and women enjoying ice cream in the open air café at Rockefeller Center. In the winter the tables were placed indoors, and the patio was turned into an ice-skating rink. To strains of Strauss and Delibes skaters pirouetted for the delectation of both the café customers, enjoying their coffee and desserts inside, and pedestrians stopping to gaze from above. My sense of alienation had not disappeared – this still was not my country - but it abated: New York, after all, was not provincial Los Angeles. And I was getting older.

My gradual "Americanization," however, did not impinge on my social life. My two best friends were the brothers Weinreich - Uriel, about a year older than I, and Gabi (Gabriel) a year younger. They were the sons of a distinguished scholar and linguist, Max Weinreich, head of the Jewish Scientific Institute YIVO, the citadel of Yiddish learning and scholarship founded in Vilna in the 1920s. YIVO, and the Weinreichs with it, had moved to New York during the war. The boys' mother Regina was a Yiddish teacher from Vilna, as warm and outgoing as Max was severe and not readily approachable.

Uriel inherited his father's scholarly proclivities, and in fact became a world famous linguist before his death from cancer at the age of 42. He and I became close friends, taking long walks, talking about everybody and everything, including hopes for the future (many), and our erotic adventures (few). We also composed and dedicated sonnets to each other, much like heroes out of some 19th century German *Bildungsroman* – all rather adolescent, but exciting nevertheless.

Gabi was quite different – full of humor, cheerful, imaginative, brilliant like his brother but choosing as his fields music and the sciences. (At his high school graduation, he played on the school organ a toccata he wrote for the occasion.) We were close too, but my relationship with him was probably not as "soulful" as it was with Uriel. Years later Gabi, who married a gentile woman, began studying Christianity, which led to his becoming a Episcopalian priest with his own congregation. To most of his friends this was a major shock. I, however, found it typical of Gabi's total unpredictability. In fact, his conversion did not entail any rejection or condemnation of his roots and one-time cultural milieu. In his own way he sees himself as both Jewish and Christian, a tricky combination no one but my friend Gabi could manage. We do not often see each other these days, but Yiddish remains our natural language, in emails or conversation.

The three of us – Uriel, Gabi and I – spent much time in each other's company, having discovered common traits and talents, such as for writing music and light verse. Eventually we embarked on writing a comic operetta, for presentation in the summer of 1943 in the Yiddish-oriented Camp Boiberik, situated near a lake not far from Poughkeepsie, New York. We all wrote both words and music, and Gabi, who I think had actually done some serious study of music, such as composition and theory, set the songs to piano accompaniment. I played the lead role, and a very pretty girl whom I secretly adored played the heroine. Lucky me! My part called for rescuing her from drowning. That was the only time I had her in my arms: she slender, sparkling, both of us shivering from the cold water poured on us back stage by an energetic member of the cast.

We called our operetta *shmerl nar in boiberik* (Shmerl the Fool in Boiberik), the title borrowed from a famous Yiddish book for children. (Boiberik was a fictitious town in Sholem Aleichem's works.) In addition to the usual camp activities, we took charge of the campfire programs and the operetta. I spent two happy summers there, acting and composing, falling in love, savoring sex, suffering the first pangs of rejected love and jealousy, then writing mournful poems no one but a few select friends were allowed to see.

In between, of course, was school. I liked Clinton High School, especially after I was transferred to the intellectually elite "Honor Classes." Once our English teacher asked who had read Romain Rolland's *Jean Christophe*, a multi-volume novel quite popular among left-wing readers in Europe (Rolland had been a pacifist and a fierce critic of World War I). I was the only one to raise my hand, quite proud to prove so exceptional and earn the teacher's compliments.

In another class, I had to write a paper on a subject altogether out of my ken - namely, "Architecture in Colonial America." (My classmates had already snapped up more congenial subjects on a day I was absent from school.) "This will prove be a useful exercise for you," said our teacher, a pleasant and pretty young woman, "when you enter college" – a prescient comment, as I was to learn. Still, I didn't know architecture from aardvarks. I sat for hours in the library looking up words like "cornice," "beading," "fluting," "dormer," and the like, in addition to mastering some knowledge of early American history, equally terra incognita for me.

My charming teacher generously gave me a "B plus" for the paper, although I still - cramming notwithstanding - knew next to nothing about the subject. The experience, however, did indeed prove a boon in college, where on two occasions I was expected to write papers on unfamiliar topics - one on Soviet physics and the quantum theory, and one on Prokofiev's piano music for children. The latter proved more enjoyable, as it involved long hours at the New York City Music Library somewhere on Fifth Avenue, listening to a great deal of Prokofiev, and occasionally to other composers as well. Prokofiev to this day remains one of my favorite composers.

The years 1941-1944, which I spent as a student first in Los Angeles and then in New York, were the years of the Final Solution, when Hitler's plan to exterminate European Jewry was first approved at Wahnsee and then implemented in Auschwitz, Treblinka and the like. Extermination camps with gas chambers sufficiently refined to asphyxiate 1200 men women and children at a time, crematoria large enough to cope with as many bodies as they received from the gas chambers - all these and more were among the supreme technological and social engineering achievements of the German Reich during those years. The SS Einsatzgruppen shot and buried thousands of Jews in the hamlets and towns of eastern Poland, Belorussia, Ukraine, and the Baltic states, as did the "Ordnungpolizei" (regular police) and killing units formed in Nazi-occupied territory.

How much public knowledge was there about this enterprise and how much understanding? As I look back at that period, it is clear to me that the Bundists in the States were better informed than most about the magnitude of the Final Solution, about the vast number of Jews dying in the ghettos of starvation, typhus and other illnesses, and the refusal of the comparatively well-armed Polish underground to extend any significant aid to the Jewish resistance groups being formed in, for instance, the Warsaw ghetto.[3]

Socialist-Zionist groups were as horrified by the ongoing carnage as was the Bund and as anguished by their inability to do anything about it. But the Bund had a larger membership than any other socialist group, continued to maintain contacts with the Polish socialists, and had a strong and remarkably dedicated representative in the Polish Government in Exile in London. In July 1942 the Bund's representative, Artur Zygelbojm, received from Warsaw the first detailed report of the annihilation of the Jews, which made abundantly clear the Nazi intention of total annihilation of European Jewry (the turn for the rest would come later, the Nazi strategists assumed). Zygelbojm did all he could to alert public opinion to what was going on, and get the Western powers to take steps to stay the hands of the executioners. Urgent meetings with British and other Allied political leaders, pleas, speeches, public meetings, newspaper letters, radio interviews - all proved futile. For various reasons now documented by historians, both Washington and Westminster judged his first report "unreliable," though its only inaccuracy consisted of the fact that since the total number of victims kept increasing from week to week, by the time they read his report, thousands more Jews had been gassed or shot.

Finally, one day in June 1943, after the Warsaw Ghetto Uprising was crushed, as the ruins of the houses lay smoldering against an empty sky and with millions of Jews already shot or incinerated, a despairing Zygelbojm committed suicide - in the hope, as he put it in his final letter, that his death would perhaps accomplish what in his life he could not: namely, to save at least some of his people. Vain hope. The letter became but one of so many minor entries in the annals of Jewish resistance.

I still remember reading *The New York Times'* story about Zygelbojm's suicide, which appeared not on the first page (as I in my naïveté thought it should) but somewhere on page eight or nine. Already overwrought, as were all others in our circle of friends and acquaintances, from children to grownups, by the news of the past few weeks, as well as by the measly coverage of the mass murders by the English-language media, stunned by the indifference to the catastrophe displayed by my school mates and indeed it seemed to me by everyone I saw on the bus, in the subway or on the street, I kept asking myself whether there was anything, anything I could possibly do, if only to assuage some of the dull pain in my chest.

And so I made a decision: to write a letter to the principal of my high school, asking for a day or at least an hour of mourning for the thousands of Jews being slain in Poland and as an expression of solidarity with the young men and women fighting the Nazi troops without any real hope for survival. I drafted a letter in long hand, and then, after showing it to a friend from one of the "honor classes," I retyped it on the Underwood typewriter given to me by my parents after I had successfully finished the typing class in my Los Angeles school. Then I walked into the school office, and with my heart beating wildly, handed over the letter to the secretary, asking her to pass it on to the principal, whom I remember as tall and thin, impeccably dressed and sporting long gray sideburns.

His reply arrived the following morning. With exquisite politeness, the principal told me that he was touched by my letter as well as by the tragedy I described. He could not, unfortunately, accede to my request lest it set a precedent for similar requests in the future.

My father, who read both letters, smiled sadly and told me not to take it too much to heart: the principal, he said, could not be expected to act otherwise. But I felt crushed. The man's response, I felt, showed that indeed no one cared about what was happening in Poland. Something unspeakable was taking place practically before our eyes (for by mid-1943, it was devastatingly clear what Auschwitz and Majdanek and Treblinka were all about), but none of the powers fighting Nazi Germany was willing to do anything about it. Auschwitz would not be bombed (but Dresden would!), the Bermuda and Evian and other international conferences were exercises in futility and hypocrisy, as were the numerous "emergency committees", "rescue proposals", and solemn promises made by the Allies. A speedy military victory, said President Roosevelt, was the first priority; other matters would come later. Millions of people were being massacred, buried in soil that for years afterwards still yielded discolored blood and human bones, the crematoria were working non-stop - and the Allies would do nothing to stop it. Nothing.

But life, as they say, goes on, and so did my life, though more bifurcated than ever before. School, books, new American friends, movies, occupied one part, and my Yiddish-speaking friends from Poland, banded together in the "Club of Jewish Youth from Poland" (later renamed so we could accommodate some "natives," too) the other. We engaged in lively discussions, sang songs, and occasionally staged performances for parents and friends, such as puppet-shows, plays, and celebrations in honor of Yiddish writers, past and living (Reizen, for one), all produced by ourselves, without supervision of adults, though for a time the teacher of the Workmen' Circle School, whose premises we used, acted, at our request, as an "advisor."

The two lives I was leading, one of dull, steady grief and the other of the mundane satisfactions and irritations of everyday life, were not necessarily discrete. Often they impinged upon each other. For some reason - I cannot remember exactly how this came about at a time when my English was still far from perfect - I became first a member of the editorial board and subsequently "Literary Editor" of De Witt Clinton High School's remarkably fine journal *Magpie*. (The staff was composed entirely of students, but under the firm if gentle control of a teacher, Mrs. Whalen, a pleasant woman in her mid-forties.) Since I was to spend a good part of my adult life as an editor, the stint at DWC seemed rather prescient. I was shown all the submitted pieces and asked for my comments, though the ultimate judge, after the other editors had been consulted, was Mrs. Whalen. She openly respected if not indeed admired my gifts as a writer.

With such encouragement, I felt I ought to write more, and accordingly submitted to *Magpie* several short stories and reviews; they were, *mirabile dictu*, promptly accepted. Leafing through them now, I see that the topics I selected bore distinctly on my "second," melancholy life: one short story, for instance, dealt entirely with the Warsaw Ghetto. Upon rereading it more than half a century later, I am astonished to find that I understood that moment in history about as well as I do now, after years of reading on the subject. So perhaps my life was not as bifurcated as I thought.

9

The Army and Americanization

Graduation and Citizenship. Army Chaos. Loneliness. Ominous Rumors. Fort Knox Hospital. Jim Crow. Basic Training Manqué.

On June 28, 1945, I bid farewell to my high school, along with about three hundred other students, many of whom brought their parents and assorted relatives to join them in celebrating the occasion. The ceremony took place in the school's auditorium, festooned with flowers and suitable slogans. After intoning the national anthem and then, with considerably more zeal, our high school hymn ("Clinton, oh, Clinton, ever to thee…"), one student after another stepped up to the stage, where at a green cloth-covered table stood the school's principal flanked on both sides by several seated teachers, all looking solemn, though breaking into an encouraging smile at any patently nervous students. The principal shook each student's hand and presented him with a attractively embossed diploma, while muttering a few words about the historic significance of this occasion, and then wished him Godspeed.

The principal's words were still ringing in my ears exactly twenty four hours later, when I found myself in a bus filled to the brim with young men about the same age as I. That morning, at a Bronx courthouse, we were all inducted into the U.S. Army. The ceremony was remarkably brief and simple, a stark contrast to the solemn ritual most of us experienced only a day earlier. The bus was taking us to Fort Dix, New Jersey, one of the largest military camps in the country, about two hours' drive from New York. Ahead lay ten weeks of arduous basic training, that collective baptism designed to convert mamas' boys into hardened combat-ready men. Or so we thought.

I didn't know a single person on the bus, and though in the four years since coming to the United States one would have though I had acquired sufficient experience to revise my supercilious view of the average American as "boorish", "primitive", "ignorant," all epithets calculated to prevent me and many of my European friends from coming to terms with reality, I hadn't, quite. As I looked around, I was struck by the ease with which all my co-travelers, as fresh out of high school as I, seemed to have abandoned the conventions of normal everyday language in favor of unending variants of the word "fuck:" "fuck up," "fuck off," "fuck you," "fuck around," "fucking difficult" or "fucking easy," and so on and on. The glee with which they bandied it about suggested something in the nature of a collective rite of passage, an audacious affirmation of newly achieved maturity.

My companions were mostly Jews, with a sprinkle of Italians, Irish and Hispanics: no Negroes, as they were then called, in the still-segregated army. The din was overpowering and persisted all the way to the gates of Fort Dix, finally tapering off as the bus drew up to a barrack with an American flag mounted in front of it. Another bus-load of recruits arrived shortly thereafter and a few minutes later a young first lieutenant greeted us and proceeded to read out our names. As each one of us responded with a brisk "present!" he was told to move to one end of the barrack or the other. The smaller group, in which I found myself, consisted exclusively of foreigners - Italians, Hispanics, East Europeans, Scandinavians – all, to our surprise, about to be sworn in as U.S. citizens. Another ceremony in the course of two days, with even less pomp and circumstance than our induction, let alone my graduation! Evidently, in a rush to get the new soldiers into the system, the authorities preferred a ceremony short on rhetoric and fuss. And so within half an hour I was clutching yet another formal document, handed to me by a smiling captain, attesting to my new status as a full-fledged citizen of the United States of America. Stunned, I barely managed to say "thank you" before joining the others.

This brings to mind my father's citizenship hearing several years later, when I was a student at the City College of New York. One day my father asked me to accompany him to a judge's office where he was to receive the citizenship papers he had applied for several years earlier. I was shocked to find the judge who would determine whether or not my father deserved the honor of U.S. citizenship coarse and patronizing. Keeping his eyes fixed on the pile of papers before him, he asked my father a few questions about U.S. history and institutions, subjects my father and I had in fact gone over a few days earlier - the names of the first five American presidents, for instance. Faced by the judge's offensive demeanor, my father got flustered - a display of weakness, I thought, vis-à-vis so detestable a man - but managed to produce the right answers. The judge mumbled something, and called for the next applicant. For a few minutes, on the street, I walked silently at my father's side, mortified by his behavior. Aware of my distress, he tried to turn the encounter with the judge into a joke. It fell flat. It wasn't until years later that I realized how offensive my judgmental attitude was, and how it must have compounded my father's sense of humiliation.

Another Bundist, the distinguished historian, I.J.Trunk, had a rather different experience – at least according to Bundist legend. Unlike most of his fellow wartime immigrants, Trunk, a somewhat bearish looking man suffering from poor eyesight and known for his quixotic behavior, never bothered to learn English properly. When he received the notification to appear for his citizenship test, he took along a translator, a youngish Bundist with a serviceable knowledge of English. The judge posed one of the standard questions, asking Trunk to list some of the freedoms guaranteed in the Bill of Rights. Trunk mentioned three: freedom of assembly, of expression, of religion. The judge was pleased and asked Trunk whether he could cite any others, to which Trunk gruffly replied, *"far mir iz es genug"* (for me, that's enough). This apparently so flummoxed the judge that he promptly pronounced Trunk a U.S. citizen, and without further ado bid him good-bye.

My own induction into the ranks of new citizen-soldiers was neither humorous nor demeaning; it was simply matter-of-fact. We were, most of us, far more excited about the prospect of training: how to handle a rifle; how to crawl under barbed wire without getting ripped to shreds; how to "look smart" when so ordered. A burly sergeant soon disabused us of any romantic notions. We were all in Fort Dix, he told us, to type the "separation papers" for the thousands of GIs returning from Europe now that the war there was over. How long we were expected to do it, he had no idea. Maybe a few weeks, maybe a few months... In the meantime, he added menacingly, we were to comport ourselves as befitted "proud soldiers of the United States Army."

Thus began one of the most bizarre periods of my life. As if to confirm the sergeant's vague, slightly sinister warning, it lasted not a few weeks, not a few months, but an entire year, from the summer of 1945 to the summer of 1946. During all this time, work at the "separation center" (as Fort Dix came to be known) did not slacken: the European-front soldiers were followed by those stationed in the Pacific, thousands of eager GIs clamoring to go home.

My fellow-recruits and I never knew exactly how long this tour of duty would last, nor did our queries, directed at the odd non-commissioned or commissioned officer, ever yield any light on the matter. The morning after our arrival, we were told to proceed to a large hall filled with about two hundred desks, each equipped with an office chair and typewriter. This sunless and soulless place housed us for eight hours a day, from 9am to 5pm, five days a week, month after month after month. Each of us received a bundle of "separation papers;" we had to fill in the necessary data and affix our initials at the bottom of each document. At about 10:30 the Master Sergeant at the main desk, a brawny New Jerseyite by the name of Antonio Pappassergio, would blow his whistle, which meant that we had twenty minutes to do whatever our hearts desired. What all of our hearts desired every single morning, it turned out, was a brisk walk to the nearby PX, there to help ourselves to a coke and a candy bar (I favored Baby Ruth bars, delectable concoctions of chocolate, molasses and peanuts), all for ten cents. Some of my fellow typists would also buy a carton of cigarettes, which I recall cost two dollars, that is, twenty cents per pack. (A bargain, I decided

- and soon succumbed to the temptation.) Upon returning to our desks, we would be handed another batch of documents and in the afternoon yet another, and so on, every day. As summer turned into autumn and then winter, the daily pile of documents began to shrink, so eventually we would spend the mornings sitting at our desks with nothing to do except perhaps write letters or read the comics most of my co-workers adored.

Our lives, at least initially, were remarkably free of the regimentation we had expected. Once we finished working, we were entirely on our own, with no discipline, rules or regulations to contend with. It was not until three weeks after our arrival that we were even told how to make our beds (with "hospital corners") and to sweep the floor every morning. We went about in our uniforms but *sans* ties and *sans* caps, though it was drummed into our heads that we must be dressed "like soldiers" and not "like some goddamned hobos." Eventually we donned tie and hat, and practiced saluting. It seemed a simple enough procedure, but I had some trouble mastering it. ("Hey, soldier! Yes, you! Do you know who I am? Right. And what are you supposed to do? Right! So why didn't you? OK, soldier, now show me you know how. You call that a salute? Try again. Right. Again! Right - and now get going!") It was humiliating, especially if it happened more than once (it did). At least the words "fuck you" – in fact, all expletives - were taboo among officers when addressing somebody of lower rank. No such restraints were placed on the non-commissioned officers from sergeant up. What I heard in the bus taking us to Fort Dix was the acme of good behavior compared to the obscenities that regularly issued forth from the mouths of our NCOs.

For the first few months of my stay in Fort Dix I worked hard, what with thousands of American soldiers streaming back to their families. But I had my diversions. Still a committed Yiddishist, I had mailed in a subscription to *der tog* (The Day), a New York Yiddish daily. The paper would arrive with the morning mail and invariably provide M/Sgt. Pappasergio with an opportunity to indulge himself. "Hey guys!" he would bellow. "Guess what? Brumberg just got his Chinese newspaper!" A titter would run through the hall. Refusing (outwardly) to pay the slightest attention to the hubbub, I would calmly spread the paper out on the desk and proceed to read it. It was, at least at first, a traumatic experience. But in a way I enjoyed my difference, and I certainly took pride in my dearly-bought if superficial sangfroid.

By October of 1945, M/Sgt Giorgio Pappasergio left, replaced by M/Sgt Irving Pollack, a quiet, dapper, bespectacled native of the East Bronx, a Jewish neighborhood in New York. Evidently Pollack did not find my reading a Yiddish paper cause for raucous mirth. In fact, he would occasionally approach my desk and ask in a tone at once grave and solicitous, "Anything interesting there today?" Even if I did offer some tidbit of interest, he would not linger but return to his seat of power. From the ribbons on his chest it was clear he had not spent all his tours of duty in a sunless room filled with the clatter of several hundred typewriters.

About this time, our unregimented, rather chaotic free time came to an end. Now every morning we were required to go through roll call, responding to repeated orders of "attention," "at ease" and "about face" before being marched to our work place. Marched! Exercises became obligatory three times a week: running, marching, stopping, "falling out," marching again. From time to time we were ordered to "police the area," which meant bending down and removing "everything that did not grow," from cigarette butts to chewing gum wrappers. I detested this chore; it was, I felt, little more than deliberate shabby torture. But still no sign of basic training…

For months I was horribly lonely. The temptation to get on a bus to Trenton and from there on a train to New York – to parents, to friends, to civilization – was overwhelming, though on the few occasions I yielded I ended up returning so exhausted that I felt even more desperate and morose afterwards. Happily, in late October I discovered a small office in the camp with the sign "Information and Education." Inside I found a few pleasant young men, all, it turned out, college graduates with interests not dissimilar to mine. I felt like a desert-traveler suddenly chancing upon an oasis. From that time on I would rush to my water-hole whenever I could, engaging my new soul mates in conversations on anything from the latest Hollywood film to the war, a subject otherwise curiously ignored by my regular companions. The Information and Education outfit, which did not seem to generate much activity, was eventually closed down and I returned, with heavy heart, to my fellow recruits.

This is not to say that I had no company whatever. I befriended two or three young men with whom I would go bowling outside Fort Dix, or visit a local cinema. But I hungered for "real" friends and "real" conversations, longings still shaped (as they would be for years to come) as much by my European heritage as by adolescent loneliness. In the meantime, I was astonished to learn that I'd been promoted, from "private" to something called "technician fifth grade," – and I had not yet had basic training! The sleeve of my army jacket now boasted two chevrons, with T5 emblazoned in the middle. What these "lower T grades" actually meant I never discovered. (Apparently, T/5 ranked somewhere between a PFC - private first class, one stripe, which I had skipped for some reason, and a regular corporal, two stripes). My take-home pay increased by 20 dollars a month. I could now afford two Baby Ruth bars every morning.

In spring of 1946, rumors began to circulate of our impending move to a new army base, where we would – after nearly a year at Fort Dix! - at last receive basic training. The exact destination was presumably a secret, but we soon found out we headed for Fort Knox, near Louisville, Kentucky. Two days before our scheduled departure M/Sgt. Pollack informed us that our work had come to an end; another NCO told us to pack and be ready to leave for the train at 4 pm the following day.

As luck would have it, that very day my right knee swelled up like a balloon, and I writhed in pain that neither aspirins nor any over-the-counter medicines could assuage. I dragged myself to the local infirmary, where a doctor examined me and then told me he would inform the hospital in the "place you are going to" (still cautious!) to take care of me immediately upon arrival. In the meantime, he gave me some pills that alleviated but did not fully eliminate the pain. I had to be carried by two soldiers into the bus and then into the crowded train. I hardly slept that night. The trip, as I recall, took over 24 hours. There was no place to lie down. The air was hot and fetid. Some men sat on their duffle bags, some on the seats. From time to time somebody would inquire sympathetically how I felt. The noise, at first deafening, subsided eventually, as everyone succumbed to fatigue. I kept swallowing pills, occasionally dozing off, wishing the infernal trip would come to an end.

It finally did, around five in the afternoon, to the accompaniment of loud screeching and grating of wheels and violent shaking. Two medical orderlies entered the car, calling out my name. Weakly I waved an arm, and they loaded me onto a stretcher and into an ambulance standing near the train. Not a very jolly introduction to basic training! Not that I could even think of it in my dismal condition... An hour later I was deposited in the waiting room of the Fort Knox Military Hospital, blessedly air-conditioned. A smiling nurse wrote down all the relevant information: name, rank, serial number (locked in my memory to this day!), and what I thought might be wrong with my knee. "Water on my knee," I replied, having suffered from it several years earlier, when I spent two weeks in a New York hospital and had to use a cane to hobble about for upwards of two months. At that time it was the left leg, now it was the right leg. That experience left me with a dread of having fluid drained from my knee via a huge syringe. (The nurse who wielded the syringe in New York, a tall, vivacious woman in her early 20s, bubbled over with excitement as she told me about her soldier boyfriend - "you should see his muscles!" - who would soon, she hoped, return from overseas. Easily five years younger than she, I found it difficult to conceal my erection that occurred every time she pushed away the blanket to take a look at my swollen knee; she, however, ignored entirely the perturbation taking place just a few inches away.)

The doctor in Fort Knox told me that the procedure of draining (damnably painful) was no longer in use; and that the fluid would drain away or be reabsorbed in due course, provided I stayed off my feet. "You have a torn ligament," he said, and promptly assigned me to the cardiac ward, Hall Number 3.

And so here I was, finally due for basic training, and instead lying in a bed in a room with forty or so other soldiers, immobilized for the indefinite future. One thing I realized straightaway was that I was, for the first time in my life, in the South. Kentucky was not Mississippi or Georgia, but still, Jim Crow prevailed. All nurses were white, and so were all doctors. Blacks performed menial services only. I had no radio, but my neighbor to the left, a barely verbal native of Arkansas (or maybe I just found his accent impenetrable), owned a small radio, which he let me listen to once in a while. All I could get was country music, which seemed to me hellish caterwauling. The world was still in turmoil, but I could not get any news on the radio. Eventually I was able to read The *Louisville Courier*, which was supposed to be one of the best papers in the South. Accustomed to *The New York Times* (not to mention *der tog*!), I failed to appreciate the merits of this paper, but in any case if you looked carefully you could find here and there fairly informative snippets of news. The letters in the first issue I read dealt, as I recall, with the relative merits of horse manure versus chemical fertilizer.

On his first visit to my bedside, a doctor informed me that for the next two weeks I was not to get out of the bed at all, not even to go by wheelchair to the bathroom. After two weeks, he said, provided I improved, I should be able to get around by wheelchair. In the meantime, I was to take several pills every morning (nine, as it turned out!), and not give the nurses and staff a hard time.

One of the nurses who attended to me was a scrawny peroxide blonde in her early forties, Marie. We became pretty friendly, and she decided one day to enlighten me (a New Yorker, a Jew, and something of a foreigner all rolled into one) on How Segregation Works Best. She came from a small town in Texas, Marie told me, where the population was about equally divided between whites and "niggers" (I winced). But relations between the two races could not be better, she said, since after curfew, that is after 8 in the evening, whites were forbidden to stay in "niggertown," and by the same token blacks were not to be seen outside of it. Result? Perfection. No riots, no lynchings - everyone knew his place and behaved accordingly. If the same order prevailed throughout the United States, said Marie, relations between whites and "coloreds" would cease being an issue.

So here I was, a young man of determinedly socialist principles, being apprised not, to be sure, by a fanatic racist but a good-natured woman of "moderate" views, strongly opposed to violence, on how best to regulate the relations between the "coloreds" and whites. Marie was absolutely convinced that her town validated the "separate but equal" doctrine, inasmuch as the schools in both parts of the town, the facilities, the streets, the public toilets, all were equally equipped and equally looked after by the city fathers. How could I prove to Marie that her descriptions were largely bogus, a mix of hypocrisy and naiveté, that providing equal quality paper to the toilets in both parts of town – and I doubted very much that the paper was of equal quality – hardly amounted to "equality," and that her attitude toward the "coloreds" was a form of condescension bound to insult and antagonize the latter? These were the values I imbibed from my Bundist milieu, but which Marie would regard as positively wacky. I was seething. "So this," I said to myself, "was what passed for 'equality' in this 'greatest of all countries' in the world." But after trying several times to open her eyes, I gave up. It wasn't worth the effort.

The "southernness" of my new milieu came home to me, too, via the occasional visits of missionaries who were apparently free to enter the ward and approach any patient. As a rule I tried to pretend I was asleep, but once I let myself get into a dispute with three young people, two men and one woman, spreading the good tidings on behalf of the Seventh-Day Adventist Church. They came equipped with large quantities of religious literature, including Bibles for the odd lost soul like myself. At first I listened politely to my would-be saviors, occasionally entering a demurral or question. They replied firmly but tactfully. After a while, worn out from an exchange that was bound to lead nowhere, I told them bluntly that I was a Jew and an atheist into the bargain. To my amazement, my words produced an opposite effect from the one intended. The three young people became positively elated and threw themselves into the discussion with increasing brio - for what greater reward can there be than leading a stray sinner to the Truth? Finally, I pleaded fatigue, and they took off, leaving behind a small library of confessional literature. I looked around: my fellow patients seemed not to have seen or a heard a thing.

I stayed in the hospital a total of two months, permitted to take walks about halfway through my stay. I walked to the library, which boasted a full set of Sinclair Lewis' novels. I devoured them - *Main Street, Dodsworth, Babbitt, Arrowsmith* - finding in them confirmation for all my inchoate but scornful views about America and Americans, hardly modified despite five years in this country. The Fort Knox Hospital also contained an antediluvian record player and some records, mostly country music but a few that were more to my taste: *H.M.S. Pinafore*, Brahms' Second and Fourth Symphonies, Beethoven's Egmont Overture, Dvorak's New World Symphony. I listened to the records day after day, after a while committing to memory the major themes from the Brahms symphonies and virtually all the songs from *Pinafore*. One of the chief nurses became aware of my passion for music (I used to bang on the piano at the library at odd hours of the day and night), and asked whether I would like to participate in a "talent show" with other GIs. I agreed with alacrity. I played a waltz I had written some two years earlier, as well as variations on a tune popular at that time. I knew that my efforts hardly matched the skills displayed by other GIs, all of them music students of one type or another. But I was always happy to perform, especially when my performance drew compliments from the nurse.

Towards the end of August 1946, I was told that my release was imminent. Natually, I expected to be dispatched somewhere for the long postponed basic training, but this was not to be. My stay in the hospital, it turned out, entitled me to a four week "convalescent furlough," which I could use for any purpose I desired: to go home or to a resort, to visit friends, whatever. During those four weeks I would of course receive my army pay as I did during my stay in the hospital.

I mulled over the possibilities, and finally decided that since I should soon be discharged and sent home anyway, I might as well use the furlough to revisit Los Angeles. Four years after we'd left, I relished the prospect of returning as an adult.

Of course I had not the slightest intention to spend money on an airline ticket to L.A. Instead, I went to the local small airport and found that as luck would have it, a small plane was due to leave late that afternoon for San Bernardino, California, via Tulsa, Oklahoma. I was delighted, and two hours later, small suitcase in hand, I approached the plane that was standing lonely on the field, with no other planes in sight, and spoke to the two pilots sitting nearby. Sure enough, they'd be happy to have me aboard. I climbed in. There were two seats for the pilots, and in the back there was room for at most two passengers. The pilots asked me to squeeze myself as far back as possible, so as to provide more ballast for the plane when it took off; then they entered the cockpit and several minutes later we were on our rackety way.

The ride was bumpy, and I was asked a few times to shift my weight now to the left, now to the right, but we arrived safely, three hours later, in Tulsa. I decided to splurge on a hotel, bound to be better than the filthy seats at the Tulsa Military Airport and I bummed a ride with a soldier going into town. In Tulsa most of the streets were empty; one, however, seemed packed with men all heading in one direction. The local movie theater, explained the driver, was showing the new Hollywood hit, Jane Russell in *The Outlaw*, and everyone was anxious to take "a good look at her famous tits." The streets near the theatre were plastered with huge posters of Miss Russell, which made it altogether clear that those famous breasts would stay firmly inside their tight cups, the brassiere in turn ensconced in a flimsy, tight blouse. We were still neon light years away from Hollywood's explosion of bare-all. I decided to go to bed.

At six the following morning, having been sternly warned to come on time, I was back at the Tulsa airport, eerily quiet and with nothing in sight save my trusty mini-plane and its two pilots. They looked me over with amusement - I looked about 16 years old at that time - and told me again to climb in and "make myself comfortable," a physical impossibility in that plane. Again the motor roared, and we were soon climbing up in the sky, higher and higher, finally leveling off over a vast stretch of desert followed by spectacular mountain ranges, with patches of snow and ice above the tree lines. It was a magnificent sight.

As we entered the third time zone since our departure from Kentucky, the sun seemed never to go down. It was not until the plane began its descent and landed in San Bernardino that I became aware of the lateness of the hour. We were again in a small airport, but this time tall palms surrounded us; rows of flowers spread intoxicating scents that I remembered from my year in California. I thanked the two pilots and stepped into a telephone book to make a few phone calls. My address book featured the names of several friends of my parents and myself, all of them, I felt certain, eager to meet the prodigal son and offer him that marvelous hospitality - *mishpokhedikayt* - every person raised in a Bundist milieu could expect from a fellow Bundist, familiar or previously unknown. Besides, I couldn't wait to show myself off, no longer the teenager they had known but a young man in an American army uniform sporting important looking logos on both sleeves.

As it turned out, reality lived up to expectations. The L.A. friends were indeed delighted to see me, their hospitality overwhelming, and my old friends, similarly grown-up, welcomed me. I met so many good-looking girls that I could find no time to fall in love, not even to spin a brief romance... Anyway, my principles – and inexperience – precluded brief affairs: the concept of love as something serious, pure and soul-inspiring, borrowing more from romantic Polish literature than from Marx and Engels (or Hollywood movies), held me in its thrall. Los Angeles in the summer of 1946 was one movable feast after another. I had such a splendid time that I forgot that my leave was about to expire. When I remembered, someone misguidedly advised me to send a telegram to the commanding officer in Fort Knox, informing him that I was not in tip-top shape and requesting an extension of my sick leave by one week. Of course there was no reply: the CO in Fort Knox must have thought I was soft in the head! In the end I took a bus to the San Bernardino airport, where a plane was leaving the following morning for Memphis, Tennessee. I was welcome to take one of the still available seats. By this time I realized, to my horror, that I was already three days AWOL, and that I'd used up all my money: I had no idea how I would get from Memphis to Louisville.

So there I was the following day at the miserable Memphis airport, virtually penniless, the sun beating down on me, and wondering how in God's name I could ever get out of this mess. As was my wont I confided in a soldier sitting next to me, and his advice - this time sound - was to give myself up to the MPs. The very act of voluntarily turning myself, he said, was bound to weigh in my favor if and when I should ever be brought to trial.

Scared but determined, I went to the army guardhouse and told the two MPs in the office that I was AWOL and wished to turn myself in. My sheepishness, or maybe my youth, won the amused sympathy of one of the MPs, who told me to empty my pockets, put my uniform in a duffle bag and don a pair of (oversized) fatigues. Haltingly, I asked the MPs whether they had any idea how long I would stay in the guardhouse – I probably had visions of leaving as an old man. The question aroused considerable merriment. "No idea, soldier," they said, "it all depends on the CO." In the hateful fatigues I entered the guardhouse, not a prison but a large barrack where the soldiers, mostly AWOLs plus a few accused of petty larceny, spent a good part of their days playing cards and reading comic books when not out "on detail."

"On detail," as I found out the following morning, meant marching to the dining room for breakfast (while the regular soldiers gazed at us with undisguised curiosity), and then marching from barrack to barrack collecting the large cans of litter standing in front of the barracks, carrying them onto a garbage truck that followed us and then emptying the contents of the truck into a vast adjacent field of garbage. The fumes and smells invaded your body so insidiously that when you finally returned to the guardhouse all you could think of was stripping and taking a hot shower, soaping your skin again and again until the last whiff was gone.

My fellow inmates included one boy, who looked not a day over 12 but was, I learned, 15 years old and who had run away from home (Texas, I think) to join the army. Now he was waiting for the official orders sending him back to mom and dad, probably accompanied by a sergeant, whose ticket would also come out of the boy's pay. I grew restless, once more confiding in one of my buddies, who told me (no doubt laughing up his sleeve) that as a "non-commissioned officer" I had the right to refuse to do any work until properly court-martialed. Without giving it too much thought, I approached the second lieutenant in charge of the guardhouse, a huge man with a blond crew cut, and mustered all my courage – fast leaking away – to state my case. The lieutenant looked at me quizzically and inquired as to the source of this curious notion. I stammered, he snarled, and dismissed me and my "stupid questions." Chastened and embarrassed, I returned to my bed, resolved never, never again to make such an ass of myself...

Fortunately, my orders were "cut" (to use the army parlance) the following day and I was told that a ticket had been issued for me on a train from Memphis to Louisville. A sergeant would accompany me to the train station and then release me from his care. I wouldn't do anything silly between here and Louisville, would I?

"No, sir!" I fervently (and sincerely) replied. Two hours later I was sitting in the train near a window, looking out at fields and woods and occasional wooden houses, at horses and cows speeding away into the distance. "Tomorrow basic training." I muttered to myself. "At last!"

That night, around midnight, I arrived again in Fort Knox, and went directly to orderly room 135, where a new company of recruits had just begun its ten-week basic training. When I entered the room, a sleepy looking sergeant and an even sleepier looking captain looked me over, and told me to find a bed anywhere I wanted, but to make sure to report to the orderly room every hour on the hour and sign in: name, rank and - of course - serial number. FOUR TWO TWO FOUR SEVEN EIGHT ONE FIVE! I followed orders, found an empty bed in the first barrack I entered, and fell asleep immediately. How I managed to get up every hour I cannot imagine. But I did, dragging myself from bed to orderly room and back to bed all through the night. In the morning, eyes smarting and heart beating rapidly, I reported for basic training, my long-delayed baptism into genuine American citizenship...

Well, not quite. The company to which I reported was about to start its second week of basic training and I was worried about keeping up with the others. Luckily, it turned out that the first week had been spent on the kind of drills I had gone through in Fort Dix, so I quickly caught up with the others. By the second day, however, the pace increased: long walks, with full packs, for five and seven and then ten miles, with not a cloud in the sky and our knapsacks at the end of the march soaked in sweat. Then by truck to the firing range, where we learned how to hit a target rather than the man standing to the right or left. That, I thought, was rather fun. To crawl on your stomach under barbed wire, however, was no fun at all.

Once I was told to approach a monstrously large truck, to sit down in the driver's seat and to start the motor. The truck, said the instructor, had six gears. He might as well have said it had six stars or six screws, for all I understood. The instructor seemed flabbergasted. Never, apparently, had he seen an American youngster so abysmally ignorant about automobiles. Another soldier replaced me, doing what was necessary without batting an eyelash. No doubt a farm boy, I thought to myself. Clearly, there were giant steps to overcome on my road to Americanization.

Exactly one day later, we were all given rifles and shown how to disassemble them. This seemed relatively simple. Then the sergeant barked: "And now put them together again!" Most of my fellow trainees semed to get the hang of it. Not I, however, nor one or two other *shlimazels*. After half an hour, with everyone else already off the tarmac, the other two finally succeeded, and departed. Only I remained, sitting on the hot ground, the sun beating down on me. I just could not fathom it. The sergeant took pity on me and told me I could go back to my barrack. I picked up the pieces of the rifle, handed them to the sergeant and fled.

The following morning, amazingly enough, my bacon was saved. My orders had just come through: I was to report to the orderly room to get my discharge papers. Plucked out in the middle of basic training! How opportune! I was euphoric. All night long I had dreamt about huge monsters aiming peculiar looking weapons at me. Now I was free, liberated, happy. I saluted the officer smartly as he gave me the papers, did an about-face, and was out, running to the barrack. That evening, in the train, my duffle bag resting on the rack above, I sat looking out the window, hardly able to contain my excitement. A paperback thriller lay on my lap. But I was too restless to read. At 8 am, the train pulled into Pennsylvania Station, New York City. My parents waited on the platform, smiling broadly, waving their arms and then covering me with hugs and kisses. A new life was about to begin.

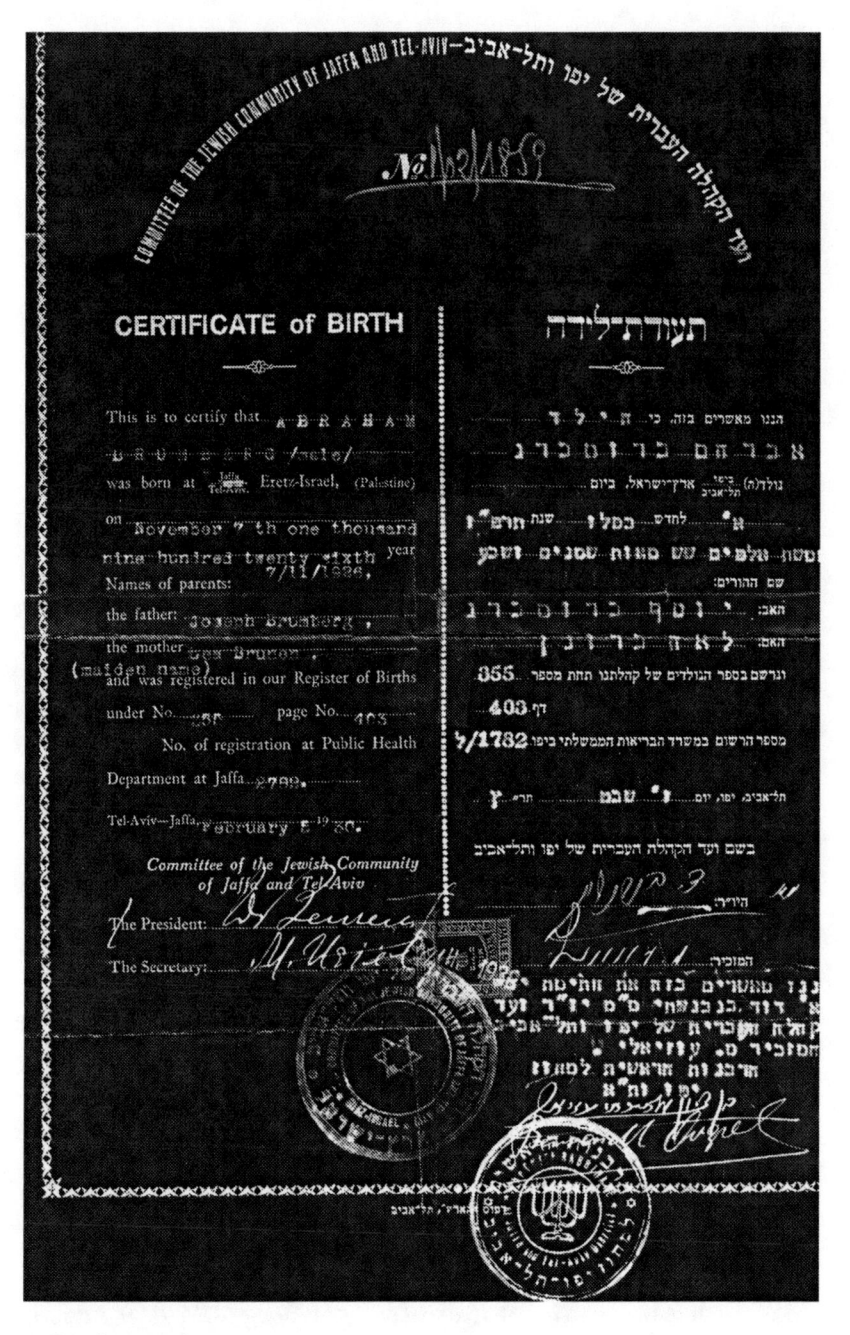

1. Birth certificate

2. Sketch of Medem Sanatorium by Yosl Berger *Medem sanatorie bukh* (Tel Aviv 1971) p. 145.

3. Meteorological station Medem Sanatorium

4. Carrying apples from our orchard (AB 1st on right)

5. Childrens' council Sanatorium

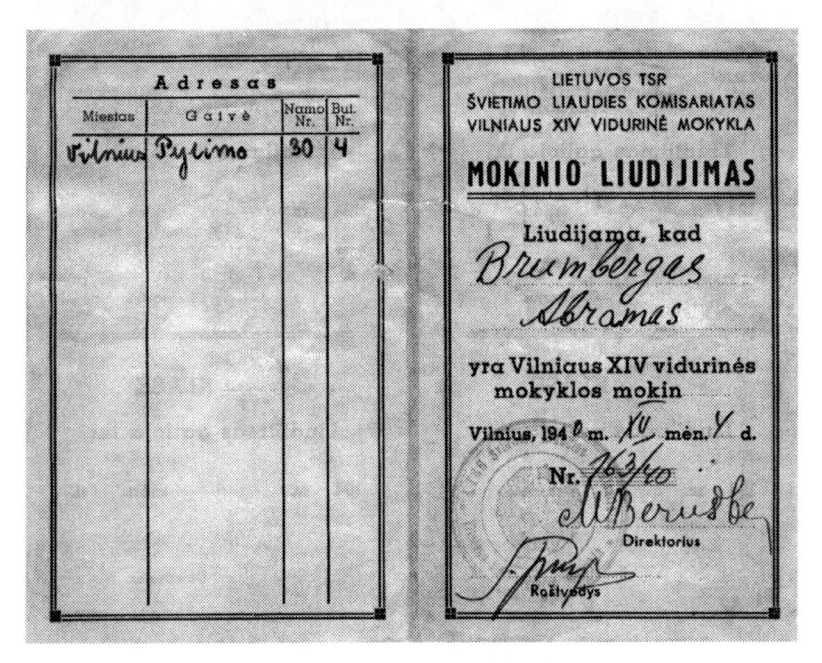

6. School ID Vilna

8. Bundists at the Kamakura Buddha in 1941 (AB 3rd from left)

9. Bundists in Los Angeles in 1941 (1st row 2nd from left my father Joseph, 2nd row 3rd from left my mother Lola)

10. Technician 5th grade AB

11. Recuperating, Fort Knox

12. Naturalization Certificate

13. AB with Uriel (middle) and Gabby Weinreich (1942)

14. AB with fellow Yiddishist Joshua Fishman (1944)

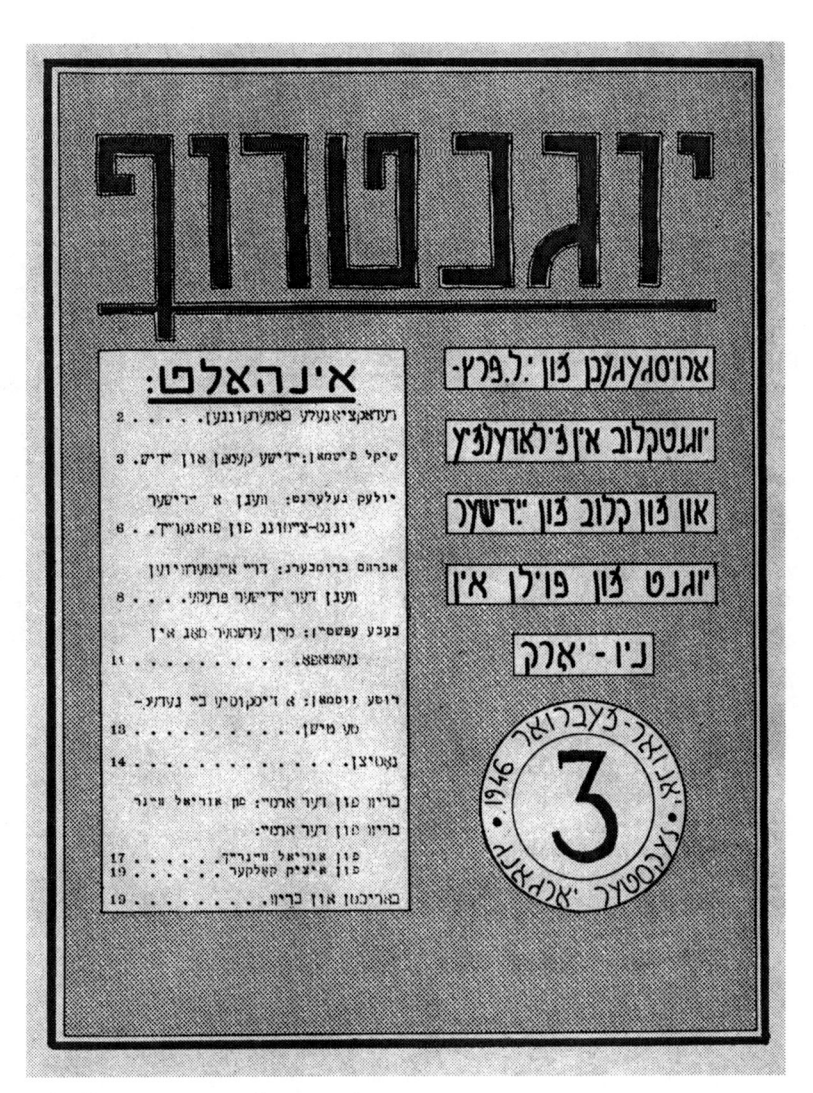

15. Cover *yugntruf* magazine

16. Actor Maurice Schwartz at CCNY (late 1940s)

17. My father and I (1954)

18. My parents (early 1960s)

19. Sovietologists, from left Unidentified, AB, Joseph Berliner, Jerzy Gliksman, Robert Tucker

20. Young professionals, historian Abraham Ascher, AB (1957)

21. Irving Howe and AB, Bellagio (1984)

22. Josephine Woll and Andrei Amalrik, Holland (1980)

10

City College and All That

*Christmas and Chanukah. Politics and student life.
Commemorating the Warsaw Ghetto. Academic discoveries.
Resign, Brumberg, resign! Singing and Skiing.
Professional presentiments.*

My first distinct memory of CCNY – the City College of New York – is of Christmas Day, 1947, although by December 1947 I had already been an enrolled student for several months. Still, everything preceding that Christmas Day fuses into one big blur: registration, the elation I felt upon learning that even as a first year student, I had a choice of courses, the first classroom hours, where I felt I was at last treated as a mature adult. All this yields in my memory to the image of a huge Christmas tree standing in the main hallway, adorned not only with the standard trinkets but also, astonishingly (to me, at least), with small Menorahs, electric five-starred lights, and a replica of an ancient *sidur* (Hebrew prayer book) right next to an equally small replica of an illuminated 15th century Bible, the two items hanging side by side in a spirit of interdenominational amity. Several hundred students surrounded the tree; a young man who turned out to be a highly popular mathematics instructor led them as they cheerfully sang "Chanukah oh Chanukah", then "Silent Night" and "Come, All Ye Faithful" – the lyrics of which, in Yiddish and English, were clearly familiar to most of the singers.

This holiday scene, then, is not what greeted me when I arrived on Day One at CCNY, but its uniquely New York flavor indelibly imposed itself on my mind. I doubt if the universities of Montana or Nebraska or even Chicago would stage a Christmas celebration like it, but for City College students, more than half of them Jewish at that time, the mixture of Christmas carols and Chanukah songs was as normal and as American as today's kiosks on Washington's National Mall, selling with egalitarian panache pizza, eggrolls, bagels and hotdogs.

Unlike most American campuses, City College was and remains an urban university par excellence. Even fewer trees adorned the CCNY campus than the fictional tree, symbol of natural life amid the concrete, growing in Brooklyn. A collection of pseudo-Gothic structures as well as other buildings of various degrees of hideousness abutted on Harlem, not the most salubrious part of Manhattan, which most students avoided by walking on side streets leading to Broadway. I took a different route. From my apartment near Van Cortland Park, I would take a bus to 231st St. and Broadway, where I would board a train, exiting at 125th St. and there take a "local" train back uptown (that is, the direction I had just come from), finally alighting at 137th and Broadway, the subway station closest to CCNY. In other words, I – like most of my fellow students – spent my hours from morning to early evening ensconced in a gray cheerless setting, whether in the subway or the university buildings. No university campus I have ever been to, as a graduate student at Yale, a lecturer or visitor, or a parent taking my children on their pre-college visits, came close to the dreary atmosphere exuded by the CCNY campus.

Two kind middle-aged ladies presided over the central library, their pleasantly calm demeanor awing us into atypical silence. Not so the other library, the cavernous Army Hall, which seemed to have been designed for continuous chatter punctuated by the angry invective characteristic of the frequent acrimonious debates between Stalinists and "YPSLs" – members of the Young People's Socialist League. At which point some hapless student bent over

City College and All That   129

his notebook would invariably beg for silence, and might enjoy fifteen minutes or so of peace and quiet – until the hubbub resumed. It was not exactly a perfect site for study and reflection. Nor did the outdoors offer any solace, devoid as it was of quadrangles or lawns where one could recline with a book in hand, or just close one's eyes for a quiet snooze.

But if tranquility was in meager supply, politics, in various forms and transmutations, ran riot at CCNY, as attested to by the volumes of reminiscences penned by former leftist students who attended City College in the 1930s, many of whom later metamorphosed into neo-conservatives or - to use one of Irving Howe's inspired epigrams – "dentists." Myself, I was part of the horde of World War II veterans who would have been unable to attend any university, even the ultra-inexpensive CCNY, had it not been for the GI Bill. Less ideologically minded than the previous generations, and with the war rather than the depression our central formative experience, the foremost aim of most of my peers was to earn good grades to prepare for the hard life ahead.

But the conflicts and crises of the post-war world could not but find an echo on college campuses, especially one like CCNY. The "cold war" replaced the grand alliance between the Western democracies and the Soviet Union. Eastern Europe was falling gradually into the Communist orbit. I remember February 1948, after the Communist coup in Czechoslovakia: hundreds of students responded to a call (whose? I can't remember) to wear black armbands in a gesture of solidarity with the martyred country of Masaryk and Benes. The horror of the East European rigged trials, with their stench of anti-Semitism, would come later, but anti-Communist feeling already ran high. Groups of various political persuasions clamored for the attention of the students. I remember among them a chapter of the Students League for Industrial Democracy (SLID), social democratic in its make up, a Catholic Newman Club (rather small), a Communist chapter under some misleading name, the Jewish students organization Hillel (large and noisy). Announcements of forthcoming lectures and events, each featuring a prominent speaker, would regularly plaster the walls.

I remember one young veteran who had lost both legs in the war but could not get his GI disabilty payments because he had once belonged to the Socialist Workers Party, a small Trotskyite group headed by one of Trotsky's former lieutenants, James Cannon. The SWP had no organization of its own on the campus, so another Trotskyite group took up the cause: the Workers Party, ideologically at odds with the SWP and headed by another former secretary of Trotsky, Max Shachtman. On that occasion the legless veteran sat in a wheel chair, the wall behind him covered with issues of the WSP paper *The Militant*, a few older comrades (obviously not students) peddling the paper at the entrance to the hall. The students, most of whom did not know an American Trotskyite from a Belgian anarchist, but indignant about what was so obviously a travesty of justice, loudly applauded every speaker, including the veteran, a plain-speaking man, not an intellectual, and more impressive for all that.

In June 1948, when Stalin launched his attack on Marshall Tito as a "degenerate imperialist" and forced the Yugoslav party out of the Communist Information Bureau (Cominform), the local Trotskyite group invited Hal Draper, an active Trotskyite, to give a talk at the College. Draper, a thin, soft-spoken bespectacled man, had no taste for rousing oratory. His speech, delivered in a class room and attended by perhaps forty or fifty students, was a striking example of lucid exposition, cool delivery and refreshing absence of demagogy. The Communists showed up in full force, heckling Draper, until he reminded them that only a short while ago they had cheered Tito as "an outstanding Marxist-Leninist" and as the leader of a spunky country refusing to yield to "American imperialism." Faced with this acidulous reminder, they eventually fell silent. Naturally Draper did not suddenly become an admirer of Tito. But his dissection of the cynicism of an international movement performing somersaults at the behest of its Moscow taskmaster was devastating. Afterwards I told Draper how much I liked his talk. "The main thing," he said, "is not to assume that you are going to convince your listeners. This rarely happens. All you want to do is to shake them up a bit... the rest will come later." A sagacious comment, I thought.

A few years later I got to know Theodore Draper, Hal's brother, as taciturn a man as Hal, and also dazzlingly in command of relevant data. He wrote several books on the American CP, and eventually became a regular contributor to *The New York Review of Books*, his extravagant footnotes indulgent perhaps, but a delight to the cognoscenti. I remember visiting him at Martha's Vineyard. A man who otherwise required utter silence for his work, Draper displayed remarkable indifference when his then-wife, a singer, practiced her scales while he was reading and taking notes in the adjacent room. We saw each other fairly frequently when I was editor of the journal *Problems of Communism*, and I recall he told me once, in 1959 or so, that if I left as editor, that would be "the end of the journal." I eventually did leave and *Problems of Communism* survived – until the demise of the Soviet Union, at any rate - but I remained forever grateful to Draper for his heady compliment.

I myself took part in another event at CCNY, an address delivered by Victor Erlich, son of the renowned Bundist leader Henryk Erlich.[4] Victor, a tall, dark-haired charming man several years my elder, was a graduate student in Russian linguistics and literature at Columbia. He accepted my invitation extended on behalf of the Hillel Foundation to deliver a talk on April 19, 1948, the fifth anniversary of the Warsaw Ghetto Uprising. Erlich's audience consisted of about two hundred students who happened to be in the courtyard at the time, plus another hundred or so who came specifically to hear him – far fewer than I had hoped for. I was hardly less disappointed than I had been in high school when the principal refused my request: as in April 1943, I found it agonizing that this tragic event failed to arouse what I deemed the requisite curiosity and sympathy among my fellow students.

I have dwelt on political events because they played so prominent a role in CCNY campus life and in my own. But my college experience was also intellectually eye-opening. I found some of the courses genuinely revelatory, including an introductory course on ethics and a European intellectual history taught by Hans Kohn, the great historian of nationalism, who had just moved to CCNY from Smith College. Kohn, a heavy-set man and a mesmerizing speaker, had what I believed to be a deliberately cultivated Czech-German accent: "naytchurally" was his favorite boomed utterance. At one class, I sat next to a friend, Paul Kreisberg, both of us chatting animatedly while Kohn lectured. Kohn paused, looked at me and at Kreisberg, pointed his finger at me and said: "This man knows a lot. But I know more!" We shut up.

I took a course on painting, about which I knew next to nothing and which focused on pictorial art as a mirror of social reality. The teacher, Jacob Landy, had a robust sense of humor, and spiced his lectures with testy remarks about, and apposite illustrations of, Soviet "socialist realism:" my favorite was a painting of Stalin applauding himself. A course on the history of the First World War helped me see both its monstrous carnage and the hope it inspired of bringing about a lasting peace and a new, just order in Europe.

At the same time, how comforting it was to learn about those socialists and communists - my distaste for the latter notwithstanding - who constituted the brave if ineffectual "Zimmerwald Left," a group of Bolsheviks and left-wing socialists who at a meeting in the Swiss town of Zimmerwald in 1915 adopted a resolution condemning the war and urging the proletariat to rise against their "imperialist governments." The "patriotic" socialists voting for war credits to be used to kill fellow socialists (and others) huddled in trenches and underground tunnels inspired in me nothing but detestation. Thus the principles of my socialist upbringing conditioned my responses to so much of what I studied.

Not all courses appealed to me, of course. Mathematics proved no less exasperating in college than it had in high school. The requirement to take two years of exact sciences made me despair, so much so that I went pleading to the dean of Student Life to release me from it. Short, plump, with a silken voice and a reputation as an aggressive homosexual, he heard me out and tried to convince me that the requirement was entirely for my own good. Eventually he conceded defeat and allowed me to take only two courses, one semester each, instead of four. (I chose physics and geology, the latter because I knew it involved long walks through Central and Prospect Parks.) My fellow-students greeted my semi-victory with incredulity. "You should tell us the truth," one of them said, sardonically, "The Dean sat you down on his lap, petted your head and asked you to tell him honestly what bothered you - right?" I tried to bear the general laughter with dignified disdain...

I also decided to take a course on short-story writing, taught by an eccentric short, squat middle-aged man, Theodore Goodman. I had always excelled in my writing courses, so I thought I might try my hand at a few short stories. I was proved dismally wrong.

Professor Goodman returned my first effort with a bold D on top of the first page. The second (based clumsily on my first impressions of the United States back in 1941) also merited a D, plus the remark: "I urge you to resign." Appalled, I asked Goodman to let me speak to him in his miniscule office. He agreed, and a day later I was approaching his cubicle when I saw him approaching from the other end of the corridor. He stopped, pointed his finger at me, and bellowed, "Resign, Brumberg, resign!" - whereupon he turned on his heels and headed in the opposite direction. Stopped dead in my tracks, in a state of shock, I mumbled, "But professor..." But he was already out of earshot. That afternoon I went to the administration office and dropped the course. (Some time ago, while rummaging through my papers, I came across that fateful short story. Exactly as I remembered: "I urge you to resign, Brumberg - W. Goodman." He was right.)

The years I spent at City College were in some respects among the most influential years in my life, within campus and outside it. Outside, I devoted hours without end to Yiddish-related activities. I did not excel in sports, but enjoyed volleyball and swimming during the summer, skating and skiing during the winter. The ski slopes of New York, Massachusetts and Vermont offered fabulous delights, of the *apres-ski* variety no less than of the real thing. In addition, I joined the American Youth Hostels and went hiking with friends on the Appalachian and Horseshoe Trails in New York and Pennsylvania.

Our first trip to Pennsylvania Dutch country was full of surprises. We first came to a hostel owned by a young German-American couple (Dutch being a deformation of Deutsch), pleasant but determinedly earnest. This we found out when they insisted on giving us an hour-long lecture on the Pennsylvania Dutch, the Amish, the Mennonites, their life styles, dress, traditions, religious beliefs, foods, and so on. After the lecture - enlightening if pedantic - the hosts bid us good night and showed us our sleeping quarters: it was clear we were expected to make an early night of it. Boys were directed to one bedroom, girls to another. None us realized that our gracious hosts had locked us up for the night. This became clear towards morning, when some of us headed for the toilet facilities only to find the doors under lock and key! Luckily we were liberated fairly quickly, and cheered up at the sight of the charming horse-driven buggies used by the Amish, more severe in their habits than the Mennonites, which we came across as we headed back to the Horseshoe Trail. Luckily, too, the hosts of the other hostels on our four-day itinerary, all farmers or small landowners, turned out to be friendly but unobtrusive, happy to help but mercifully devoid of the proselytizer's zeal displayed by our first hosts.

I liked one family in particular: Herr Hagel (pronounced Hegel, like the philosopher), Frau Hagel, plus daughter and son Hagel, the family originally from Swabia. Several of us, including a college friend of mine who himself had emigrated from Germany just before the war, made it our habit later when in that area always to stop at the Hagels. When he saw us come Mr. Hagel would go into the garden to dig up some long white radishes for us. My friend and I were ecstatic: at that time, before Japanese daikon became popular, you could not get such radishes in any grocery store. Home, we exulted, just like home (*drueben!*, our hosts concurred). On one memorable Thanksgiving three of us, my friend from Germany included, arrived at the hostel bearing a goose, which we thought a fine alternative to turkey. We put the goose in the oven and then light-heartedly set out for a hike. When we came back, hours later, dark smoke was billowing from the chimney, and Frau Hagel was desperately trying to clean up the oven and kitchen. Nothing but charred bones remained of the bird. We were mortified. Many years later, my wife and I were driving around in the same area, and turned into the Hagel drive; the house was much as I remembered it. A thin woman came toward us; I immediately recognized her as the one-time teen-aged daughter I knew years ago. I introduced myself, and asked her about her parents. "Father," she said, "passed away some time ago, but Mother" - she pointed at the porch where an elderly woman was sitting on a rocking chair - "is still very much alive." I told her I didn't want to bother her mother, but could she please ask her whether she remembered my name. The daughter obliged and came back delighted: "Yes, she does remember you and wants to see you." My wife and I went up to the porch. "Herr Brumberg," she said, smiling broadly, "the goose man!"

German signs were still ubiquitous in that area. I remember huge ads for a local beer: "*Ist das nicht ein Schnitzelbank? Ja, das ist ein Schnitzelbank! Ist das nicht ein schoenes Ding? Ja, das ist ein schoenes Ding. Ist das nicht Old Reading Beer? Ja, das ist Old Reading Beer!* Why all this made me homesick for Poland I didn't quite understand. But like Herr Hagel's radishes, it did...

The Amish and Mennonites pursued their own way of life, teaching the first five grades of elementary schools in their one-room schools, fending off the insidious influences of their secular surroundings, such as electricity, telephones and the like. As many of them still do, although tourism has substantially marred the serenity of Amish life, at least on the surface. More than half a century ago Ephrata, New Holland, Bowmensville, Brickerville - villages I loved to visit - were part of a vibrant world; I am glad to have seen it before it disappears.

When I try to take stock of the changes in my life and the new paths I mapped out during my college years, I am struck, first, by the extent to which my intellectual horizons widened. The course on ethics, for instance, taught me how many ways one could think about or pose a question, ways that - perhaps as a result of my somewhat blinkered socialist upbringing - had not occurred to me earlier. Consciously or not, I was being propelled towards my eventual profession, Sovietology. For my physics course I wrote a paper on "The Soviet attitude towards Quantum Theory," a subject I knew absolutely nothing about, except that Stalinist ideology perceived it as a "capitalist anti-socialist weapon," and had eliminated any trace of it from university textbooks. I still knew nothing when I delivered the paper, but was delighted to see a B+ on the first page when my teacher returned it to me. In a course on music I decided to write a paper on Prokofiev's piano music for children, and spent delightful hours listening to them in the main branch of the New York Public Library located on Fifth Avenue.

Were politics involved? Of course. Prokofiev, like many of the best Soviet composers, was hounded by the NKVD. In 1948, he along with many other composers and writers was condemned by the Secretary of the Central Committee of the CP, Andrei Zhdanov, for engaging in "formalist" and "petty-bourgois deviations." He was forced to accommodate Stalin's megalomania in the opera *War and Peace*: the first act accurately follows Tolstoy's epic, but the second, portraying Kutuzov leading the troops against Napoleon's army, clearly glorifies Stalin's official role in the "Great Patriotic War." Prokofiev died, as it happened, on the same day that Stalin died, March 5, 1953. The Russian papers carried nothing about it for several days before finally printing a five-line obituary, and it took Prokofiev's family a week to arrange his funeral.

I remember a class at City College on, of all things, folk music, extremely popular in the 1940s in part because of the wartime left-wing enthusiasm over the alliance with the Soviet Union. Pete Seeger was a favorite, though not of mine: I considered him an apologist for Stalinism. The singers, leftists and otherwise, appeared in Carnegie Hall and Town Hall in Manhattan, occasionally at midnight. I went to as many concerts as I could, learning many of the songs into the bargain.

One performer, quite unique, was Richard Dyer-Bennett, his voice an immensely flexible high tenor. He specialized in American, Scottish, German and Irish ballads, and unlike the jeans and plaid flannel shirts favored by the populists, he invariably appeared on stage in formal dress. I also loved silky-voiced Josh White, and the older, far gruffer Huddy Leadbelly, the former Mississippi killer rescued from the chain gang by the American folk song collector and specialist Alan Lomax. After inserting his false teeth into his mouth, Leadbelly would sing spirituals and his own songs to the accompaniment of a 12-string guitar. Needless to say, neither of those two sported the kind of clothing favored by Richard Dyer-Bennett.

In my City College course on folk music, I angered many of my peers when I reported, from my own observation and reading, that after working long, hard days with only a piece of sausage and a swig of vodka to keep them going, the Soviet masses had no time or patience to create folk songs. Instead, the party-composers created songs, not folksongs in origin but often becoming quite popular among ordinary people, the mendacity of the song lyrics notwithstanding. I had in mind such lyrics as those written for the 1936 film *The Circus* and its "Song of the Motherland:" "Spacious is my native land... I know of no other where a man can breathe so freely" (*shiroka strana moya rodnaya... Ya drugoy takoy strany ne znayu, gde tak volno dyshet chelovek*). Many of the so-called Russian folk songs, I said defiantly, are written by the same kind of scribblers who produce no less phony "happy endings" for Hollywood films. I enraged equally my Stalinist and my Stalinoid classmates (the difference between the two categories was important), who charged that my anti-Communist views rendered my testimony worthless.

One final political squall at City College comes to mind. In 1949 two faculty members, William E. Knickerbocker and William C. Davis, were both accused of racism, Knickerbocker for anti-Semitic remarks, and Davis for preventing Black students from moving into the dormitory he ran, Army Hall. The campus was in turmoil. Every day, students stayed out of their classes, parading with huge banners reading "Don't be Asses! Don't Go to Classes!" and the like. The Communist students organized energetically, claiming this cause as part and parcel of the "revolutionary struggle" they waged in behalf of the world's "proletarian" and "progressive" masses headed by the Soviet Union. The demonstrations culminated in a strike demanding action against the two racist professors. In the end Knickerbocker was allowed to resign quietly about a year later. Davies was asked to leave, and found himself a job somewhere else.

At that time I was active in an organization called "Federation of Yiddish Youth Clubs" which included clubs of various political persuasions, including one Communist club. I wrote occasional articles for the Yiddish daily *der tog* (The Day). The editor asked me to write about the events at CCNY, and I wrote a fairly long piece, showing that although most of the students were in favor of only a one-day strike, the Communists misrepresented it as "a continuous strike." During the strike, I ran into an ardent Communist and Yiddishist who told me he was collecting material for an article in the Yiddish Communist paper, *morgn frayhayt* (Morning Freedom). I realized that my article, which appeared first, would not please him, nor did it: he called his own piece "Renegade Dog Barks at his Progressive Friends," and claimed to have met me at the office of City College's president on the first day of the strike, where I was carrying out my supposedly "objective" research! He apparently failed to understand that by these words he was in fact admitting to using the same contaminated source for his own article... But then, consistency is the hobgoblin of small minds. My own Yiddish club's membership in the Youth Federation soon came to an end - as did my hope that one could, despite everything, find common grounds with Communists. In retrospect, it was a most useful experience.

11

Lev Davidovich

*A seminal figure. My first Trotskyite. Cannon and Shachtman.
Trotsky at CCNY. Trotsky, Wittfogel, Spies.
Browder vs. Shachtman.*

My life at the City College of New York would not have meant half what it did without the towering presence of Lev Davidovich Bronstein, or Leon Trotsky, as he is known to most people. For if there was ever a seminal figure who played a crucial role in my political education and steered me to my eventual profession – that now nearly defunct blend of history, political science, and crystal-ball-gazing known as "Russia Watching," or Sovietology – it was surely Trotsky. Trotsky cast a spell on my imagination, one that was to endure for some time after I left the gray buildings of CCNY for the greener pastures of Connecticut and Vermont.

Coming as I did from good social democratic stock, I was never a disciple of the "Old Man," as his admirers affectionately called him. The Bund's heroes were, rather, the Austrian democratic socialist Karl Kautsky and the Italian Matteo Mateotti, not Trotsky let alone Vladimir Ilyich Lenin. I was brought up in that spirit.

But still, Trotsky fascinated me. A Communist, he was loathed by Stalin, who first banished him from the Soviet Union, then pursued him with maniacal passion from country to country (with the complicity of Western countries), and finally succeeding in having him killed by a Soviet agent who posed as an follower of Trotsky in order to drive an ice pick into his brain on August 20, 1940, in Mexico City. Despite Stalin's Herculean efforts to recast Trotsky into a bitter enemy of Lenin and of socialism, Trotsky was in fact throughout his entire life a fierce disciple of Lenin, a Keeper of the Flame. And he fought Stalin and exposed the monstrosities of Stalin's rule more effectively than anyone else.

In the mid 1930s, Trotsky was the chief defendant *in absentia* in a series of trials held in Moscow. The accused, all venerable Communists, confessed to grotesque charges, from spying for Japan to "placing broken glass in workers' butter." Trotsky was able to refute all the shabby lies and patent fabrications before a distinguished panel of Western jurists, labor leaders, and intellectuals, headed by the philosopher John Dewey, himself far from a disciple of Trotsky's. The report of the committee was published in 1938 under the title *Not Guilty*, and it was the first book on the Soviet Union that I read in college, much to the astonishment of some of my parents' friends. "Why this interest in a piece of almost ancient history?" I recall one of them, the wife of a prominent scholar, saying to me.

The second book, given to me by my father, was *Behind the Urals - an American Worker in Russia's City of Steel*, by John Scott, one of the first in the "literature of the disenchanted." Scott was an American welder who spent five years in Magnitogorsk in the 1930s trying to provide a helping hand in the construction of a brave future, with predictably flawed results. My father, suspecting that City College was awash with youthful admirers of the "Great Experiment," thought Scott's book would prove a good antidote. He was right.

That the trials in Moscow were not exactly "ancient history" was soon illustrated by similar events in the East European Communist-ruled countries - Bulgaria, Romania, Hungary, Czechoslovakia, and to a lesser extent in Poland. The more I read about the purges and the trials the more convinced I became that they held the key to a system that started out on a utopian note and then turned into a nightmare. For what was it if not a nightmare: prominent Communists confessing to collaboration with Nazi, Fascist, and Imperial Japanese intelligence agencies? Seasoned revolutionaries acknowledging, in tandem with the prosecutors, that one single person bore responsibility for this treachery, one man orchestrated and supervised this enterprise - namely, Leon Trotsky? Why and how this could have happened tormented me, even more now that Trotsky was dead but the same grisly scenario was being reprised in Eastern Europe. Other culprits, a new *dramatis personae*, supplanted Trotsky: the "international Zionist conspiracy," the Joint Redistribution Committee (a.k.a. Zionists), Wall Street (ditto), American imperialism - all rolled into one, all constituting the evil force responsible for turning the original dream into utter catastrophe.

I met my first genuine Trotskyite even before I got to CCNY, during my army service in Fort Dix in 1945. His name was – unbelievably - Leo Brounstein. He was thin, scruffy, energetic, with curly hair and darting eyes. Roughly my own age (about eighteen), Brounstein's self-assurance captivated me. First, he seemed to know all I ever wanted to know about the Soviet Union, and second, he had a position, or a "line" on every subject, which imparted an ineffable air of authority to all his opinions and *obiter dicta*. (In fact, the phrase "a line on this subject" occurred frequently in his speech - not inadvertently, as I quickly learned. It was supremely important, he also explained, that one's views be rooted "in a firm theoretical matrix.") He had formerly been a follower of James Cannon, he told me soon after we met, the leader of the other American Trotskyite splinter group, but just a few weeks earlier had joined the followers of Max Shachtman: evidently, Cannon's theoretical matrix was wanting in some essential respects.

Cannon and Shachtman, one-time secretaries to Leon Trotsky, split in 1940. Cannon held to the orthodox Trotskyite position: the Soviet Union was a "degenerated workers' state," and should be defended, *malgré tout*, against the capitalist and imperialist world. Shachtman on the other hand maintained that there was nothing "proletarian" or "socialist" about the Soviet Union any more, and that its society constituted a new form of "bureaucratic collectivism" deserving not the support, but rather the unsparing condemnation of the "international proletariat." Leo Brounstein happily explained the arcane details of this schism, but they don't much matter: suffice it to say that altercations between the two once-fraternal leaders and their allies were bitter. Cannon continued to edit *The Militant* and *The Fourth International*, organs of the Socialist Workers Party; Shachtman, whose group first called itself Workers Party, and eventually the Independent Socialist League, began publishing a monthly called *New International*, and a weekly called *Labor Action*. Both groups were miniscule, numbering no more than two thousand members each, hardly any of them workers, most of them New Yorkers. Many years later, I learned that one of the first editors of *Labor Action* was the marvelously gifted writer Irving Howe, in later years a dear friend of mine.

(There was also, as I found out by scanning the newspaper kiosks at Union Square in Manhattan, scene of radical assemblies since the 1880s, something called a "Workers' Socialist Party," with headquarters in Canada. And the International Workers of the World (IWW), with headquarters in Seattle. And the Socialist Party. And the Socialist Labor Party. Each with its own publication. It was enough to wear down the most dedicated reader of the American left-wing press.)

In addition to his political confidence, another aspect of Leo Brounstein's life impressed me. By his own accounts he was, if not a fearless libertine, then certainly a fearlessly liberated New York Jew. I am referring to his stories of sexual derring-do - or what passed for derring-do in my eyes. With scarcely concealed pride, Brounstein told me how his girl friend would join him in the shower, there to kneel and perform fellatio, while water poured over her bent head. He described his sensations in stunning detail. I was green with envy.

And so, when I entered City College two years later, I already had an inkling of what Trotsky and the various groups that paid homage to his name were all about. More: with Leo Brounstein as my model, I had come to regard anything bearing on the subject of Trotsky with a certain amount of awe. (Liberated sex - product of a contemptuous rejection of "petty-bourgeois" values - was also, I believed, an essential attribute of a full-fledged Trotskyite.) As for Leo, he went to Chicago, and as I heard later became the head of a Shachtmanite group at the university. Then I lost track of him.

My nodding acquaintance with Trotskyism, as it turned out, stood me in good stead. When I enrolled in City College, I had no idea of what I should later do with my life. Yet one thing was clear already - that my avid interest in communism and in Russia would endure. For this I had to thank both literature and life: my Bundist upbringing, the novels of Tolstoy and Dostoyevsky that I devoured in my teens, and my bracing, not to say chilling, experience as a non-Communist youth among fervent Communist neophytes in Soviet-occupied Vilna in 1940-41. Leon Trotsky added to the mix.

In the late 1940s, many Americans were still entranced by communism and the Soviet Union. Though no longer the only "bastion against fascism," as a good chunk of the American Left regarded it in the 1930s, or later the gallant ally of the "Western democracies" in the struggle to make the world safe from Nazism, the Soviet Union was still admired by many as a country that for all its unattractive features was determined to create a stable and just society, free of the curses of capitalism (unemployment, poverty, inflation) and free, too, from such ancient vices as racism, religious bigotry and anti-Semitism. The lack of elementary knowledge about the Soviet Union of most Americans was mind-boggling. Few people had any inkling about the country's insane economic system, its reign of terror, the absence of democratic rights. (Some true believers, readers of *The Daily Worker* and of *PM* and similarly high-minded if meretricious publications, certainly knew, but thought these were all "imperfections" destined to disappear.)

It was precisely to counter this abysmal ignorance that Sovietology came into being. When I entered college, the study of the Soviet Union, later to burgeon into hundreds of academic courses, learned journals, conferences and op-ed punditry, was still embryonic. Harvard, Yale and Columbia had only recently launched special courses in Russian history, Soviet government, the history of the Communist international movement, and related subjects. The East European countries were becoming "satellite states;" the cold war was shifting into high gear. Where could one turn for enlightenment on these subjects? Unlike Germany, where *Oest Europa Forschung* had thrived as a bona fide discipline since the late 1920s, and unlike Great Britain, which also boasted several eminent specialists in this field, the outstanding American contributions (by scholars like Merle Fainsod, Alex Inkeles, and Joseph Berliner) were still in the offing. Meanwhile those of us interested in the field didn't have too many sources to choose from.

There was the slightly daft left-wing academic, Frederick L. Schuman, who thought it sufficient to know the individual rights spelled out in the 1936 Soviet Constitution (the "world's freest," in Joseph Stalin's words), and ignored their implementation – or rather lack of implementation – in real life. There were several books by David Dallin, a pedigreed Menshevik, some written in collaboration with another Menshevik, Boris Nicolaevsky. (The Mensheviks were a moderate wing of the Russian Social Democratic Party that fell out with Lenin back in 1903, who thereafter vigorously persecuted them as "right-wing traitors" and "bourgeois nationalists".) But these, like the writings of David Shub, belonged more to journalism than to scholarship, and furthermore their strong if altogether understandable anti-Bolshevik bias, however appealing to me, cast doubt on their reliability.

Dallin, Shub, Nicolaevsky and the elderly Solomon Schwarz and his wife Vera Alexandrova (the last one of the few people taking an interest in Soviet literature and literary politics) were the most prolific contributors to the Menshevik journal *Sotsialisticheskii vestnik* (Socialist Courier), published first in Czechoslovakia, then in France and now in New York, as the Mensheviks kept one bare step ahead of Hitler. Several of the journal's other contributors were more rigorous scholars than Dallin and Shub - *Sotsialistichekii vestnik* actually contained a great deal of important information on and insight into the Soviet Union - but at that time I had not yet learned Russian, so the journal was out of my reach.

Then I discovered Trotskyite writings, both by the "Old Man" himself and by his various disciples. My Fort Dix chum Leo Brounstein had introduced them to me, but in City College I read them for myself, and they were absolutely eye-opening. For this I have to thank a few Trotskyite fellow-students, some four or five young men who, like Brounstein, fascinated me with their political astuteness and supreme self-confidence. They spoke contemptuously of both "Stalinists" and "Stalinoids" (the latter another name for "fellow traveller"), and ironically about social democrats. This appealed to me as well, for my own Bundist milieu had considered Communists traitors to socialism and pseudo-fascists, while many Social Democrats were insufficiently "revolutionary" and too conciliatory towards the bourgeoisie. (The Bund had for a time belonged to the so-called "Second-and-a-Half International," which consisted of several like-minded European left-wing social democratic parties.)

And so I read Trotsky: *The Revolution Betrayed*, *The Stalinist School of Falsification*, his autobiography and his biography of Stalin. I read them avidly, finding him better than any source I had ever read on the malignant character of the Soviet system, its terror, lies, economic calamities. And though I did not necessarily buy the Trotskyites' "theoretical matrix," I was impressed by the skill with which their works marshaled the evidence and then traced some of the features of the Stalin regime back to their historical and ideological roots.

Plenty of our peers believed in Joseph Stalin as the hope of mankind, and believed too that malevolent enemies were thwarting his noble endeavors. I was eager to make my fellow-students understand that the reality of what they called "socialism" was grimly at odds with what they (and their parents) believed it to be. But this was not going to be easy. Accordingly, I turned to the works of Trotsky, and even more to the Trotskyite journal, *The New International*. Its pages provided me with the evidence - meticulously presented and powerfully argued - for which I thirsted, the weapons with which to battle my Stalinist and Stalinoid opponents. The folk song course had come and gone, but there were plenty of other battlegrounds ahead.

I did not buy all of it. Trotsky's own theories, for instance, seemed to me rather problematic in light of his own history. Had he not himself advocated banning all political opponents of the Bolsheviks, socialist or otherwise, in post-1917 Russia, and had he not proclaimed more than once his commitment to the credo, "My party, right or wrong?" Hadn't his hatred of Stalin's regime, I wondered, been dictated to a large extent by the fact that out of the party struggles in the 1920s Stalin emerged the winner and he the loser? Furthermore, I found some of his books, such as *Literature and Revolution*, much too dogmatic. Unlike most Bolsheviks, from Lenin to Stalin and Zinoviev, Trotsky was indeed imbued with an enthusiasm and understanding for the written word, yet all his judgments were couched in Marxist terms, all derived from his belief that only Marxism could explain literature's evolution. In addition, a utopian sententiousness marred Trotsky's language: in the socialist future "the average human type will rise to the heights of an Aristotle, a Goethe, or a Marx. And above this ridge new peaks will rise." Etc. This was too rich for my blood, and ran counter to Trotsky's and his disciples' corrosive skepticism toward pretentious and fatuous rhetoric in general, a skepticism I found extraordinarily appealing.

My Trotskyite friends and I would engage in long but generally friendly debates. The Shachtmanites, however great their admiration of Trotsky, had in effect jettisoned some of their earlier Leninist baggage, and were, I felt, almost democratic socialists at heart. One carefully aimed thrust, I thought, and down would topple the rest. Truth be told, I was somewhat reluctant to push my arguments too far, realizing that my collocutors were more polished polemicists than I was.

My faith in the Trotskyites' debating skills led to one dismaying experience. It was 1949, and I was taking a course on the Soviet government. Our instructor was an amiable man in his mid-forties by the name of Samuel Hendel - not a Communist, not a fellow traveller, but one who strove mightily to see both sides of every issue ("the one that was there and the one that wasn't," as Bertram D. Wolfe, once a leader of the American CP and then a fierce anti-Communist, was fond of observing).

One of the students in the class was a Shachtmanite, and both of us were becoming gradually more distressed as Prof. Hendel, in his disarming manner, presented to his students a preposterous picture of the Soviet Union. His interpretation of the Moscow Trials was, I felt, particularly grotesque. "It is of course ludicrous," argued Hendel (I paraphrase), "to think that the charges at the trials - such as that all the defendants were Japanese and British spies - were valid. Or that they had committed widespread sabotage. But it is surely not ludicrous to assume that these people, all of them Stalin's political foes, driven to despair by Stalin's authoritarian ways and not able to express their disagreement through legitimate parliamentary channels, would eventually take to conspiring against

Stalin, perhaps in their bitter hatred for the man even turning for help to some foreign powers?"

This kind of argument, my Shachtmanite classmate and I agreed, seemed logical but in fact had about as much basis as "where there's smoke there's fire." It was lunatic to think that old Bolsheviks, however great their loathing for Stalin, would conspire with fascist or imperialist states or with each other to impoverish and starve Russia, and to do away with their colleagues in power. Not one iota of evidence proved that these men, most of them imprisoned years before the actual trials began, had conspired to launch mayhem and murder. But how best to challenge him?

My classmate was like myself a refugee from Poland, with the improbable party name of "Maxwell." Maxwell didn't fit the "Brounstein" mold of a Trotskyite: he was lumpish, ham-fisted, without much of a sense of humor, unlikely to flout petty-bourgeois norms in or out of the shower. Nevertheless, Maxwell and I approached Hendel with a proposition: since Maxwell had views on the Moscow Trials distinctly different from our professor's, would he, Hendel, mind yielding thirty minutes of class time for the purpose of rebuttal? And could we do this during the next class, and then perhaps ascertain whose interpretation the students favored?

To my delight, Hendel agreed with alacrity: I was certain that he would suffer an ignominious defeat. No matter what he said, the Moscow Trials were, after all, so patently rigged, so transparently deceitful, the charges (whatever one thought of the reason for defendants' confessions) so preposterous and so effectively demolished in *Not Guilty*, and furthermore Maxwell's own grasp of the facts was so outstanding that I was certain he would win hands down.

Alas, I was wrong. When the hour came, Hendel concisely adumbrated his position, then turned the class over to Maxwell. About five minutes into the latter's discourse, I felt we were heading for disaster. Not because Maxwell failed to demonstrate the bogus nature of the charges against the defendants and not because he succumbed to Hendel's spurious arguments, but because Maxwell, who knew more about the Soviet Union than Hendel and all the students rolled into one, could not control his passions - or his English, highly accented but normally altogether serviceable.

As a result, he steadily succumbed to his own rage, frustration and, worst of all, self-righteousness. He felt the audience's antagonism, he said later; he realized as he spoke that his efforts to condense what he had learned over many years (one does not become a Trotskyite overnight) into several concise propositions were unsuccessful; and he felt that his listeners were insensitive to the human tragedy of once dedicated revolutionaries, leaders of men, war heroes, famous orators, forced to grovel before an insatiable tyrant.

Maxwell grew increasingly agitated. He stumbled, he spluttered, he raised his voice. After a while, it became impossible to know whether he was actually making sense: his accent had become impenetrable. I remember sitting there, aghast. The students began to fidget. Hendel himself looked puzzled. Finally Maxwell stopped and it was all over. There was a moment of silence, and then Hendel took a quick vote: the vast majority of the students opted for their instructor's version of the trials. Maxwell, of course, was crushed. So was I. I felt he had betrayed both Trotsky and myself. For several days following the debate, I was inconsolable.

Years later I witnessed another orator's collapse. By then, about 1960, I was already a professional Sovietologist, and in this capacity I invited a German professor by the name of Karl August Wittfogel to give a talk to the Washington, D.C. branch of what later became the American Association for the Advancement of Slavic Studies. Professor Wittfogel, then in his late sixties, had in the early 1920s been a member of the German Communist Party, and after leaving it, became an eminent Orientalist. It was then that he developed his theory of "hydraulic societies," which held that in societies whose survival depends largely on the efficacy of its large public works system (in China, its hydraulic network), political power lies in the hands of those who control these works; and that this in turn leads inexorably to a totalitarian political structure.

The theory was a bit potty, and for years nobody took much notice of it, but in the 1950's, with the emergence of works on the origins and nature of totalitarianism (by Hannah Arendt, Zbigniew Brzezinski, Carl J. Friedrich, and others) that attempted to sweep all totalitarian regimes, their distinct features notwithstanding, into one theoretical bag, Karl August Wittfogel's ideas again emerged in the open.

I met Wittfogel in his posh apartment on Park Avenue. Present was also Bertram D. Wolfe, an old friend of Wittfogel's. Wittfogel was a tall man, slightly stooped, with a pensive smile, and a devastatingly strong handshake. He was eager to meet a young man who already, as he informed me, was the holder of so much "power." (Apparently to be the editor of a journal on communism at the height of the cold war was, in Wittfogel and Wolfe's opinion, second in importance only to that of totalitarian dictators.) He sat me down, offered me a cup of coffee, and launched first into a few perfunctory questions, and then into a long soliloquy. The first part, dealing with his experiences as a professor of Chinese History, I recall as absorbing. After a while, however, the soliloquy seemed to get progressively more disjointed and incomprehensible, less an academic analysis than the ranting of an intellectual warrior battling Antichrist – that is, the Communist Menace. He "named names" (as the McCarthyite circumlocution had it) in the academic establishment: people who were, in Wittfogel's opinion, not only "leftists," "fellow-travellers," or "Soviet apologists," but outright traitors, "agents", "spies." Wolfe, nodding vigorously, obviously agreed.

Spies! I had heard accusations of "being soft on communism," "Soviet apologists" and the like, most of which struck me as demagogic, but to level outright charges of treason against well known academics (such as Arthur and Mary Wright, both distinguished Sinologists) was mind-boggling. Moreover, Wittfogel's accent – like Maxwell's – became more and more impenetrable, and his speech more incoherent. He lost me. When he finished, I remember getting up, dazed. I left shortly thereafter, after another vigorous handshake.

Nevertheless, I though that my fellow-Sovietologists in Washington might benefit from exposure to Wittfogel - and vice versa. I made arrangements, and a few weeks later Wittfogel appeared in Washington. His lecture, I recall, took place in a room at George Washington University. Few of the eighty or so people who attended – academics, students, and government officials – had ever actually read Wittfogel. All, however, were eager to hear him. Wittfogel spoke about an hour and fifteen minutes. The first half hour or so was fine. But then, as in New York, he almost imperceptibly slithered onto the subject of "agents" and "spies." The accusations came with dizzying speed. The American academic establishment, he charged, was in the hands of scoundrels ready to sell America down the river. Utmost vigilance was called for.

The audience, having recently survived the squalid McCarthyite circus, was by now inured to the ranting by vulgar rabble rousers such as the former Junior Senator from Wisconsin and his supporters in the right-wing press. And it was also accustomed to hearing the argument, made by such respectable scholars as the philosopher Sidney Hook and the subsequent guru of the Neo-Conservatives, Irving Kristol, that no one with any ties, present or past, to "fellow travelling" organizations had any business teaching classes in American universities or working for the government. Wittfogel, however, was made of different stuff. He was a genuine weirdo. The audience, baffled and offended, grew restless; they had the courtesy to applaud, slightly, but asked no questions and made for the exit as quickly as possible.

The following morning the phone rang, and Wittfogel's voice came over the wire. "Abe?" he said with that German lilt I had grown to know, "vat did you think of last night?" "Oh," I said, a bit lost for words, "it was fine, Karl, fine. The audience was extremely interested." "You don't say so!" said Karl August cheerfully, "I am so glad! You know, I did not vant to say anything nasty about anyone - vy be a sourpuss?" That last word he delivered with inimitable Teutonic intonation. I thought of all those whom Wittfogel had denounced the night before. But without being "a sourpuss!" "Yes," I agreed, "you are quite right. See you soon, Karl – goodbye." I never saw Wittfogel again. I did not think I could face him. Unlike Maxwell, who was (no doubt only temporarily) crushed by his classroom experience, Wittfogel was exceedingly pleased with himself. But neither man could, in the end, distinguish facts from murderous passions.

During my last year at CCNY, I lost some of my awe of the Trotskyites. Other influences competed, as I began to read the first Sovietological works that were appearing from the presses of Harvard and Columbia Universities, the pioneers of Soviet studies. The books were more rigorous in their scholarship than those of either the Trotskyites or Mensheviks.

Nevertheless, my infatuation with Trotsky had not yet run its course. I read now not only his own works, but books about him, such as the first of the three-volume biography by Isaac Deutscher, and books about the attempts on Trotsky's life. The first of these, published in 1948, was called *Murder in Mexico*, written jointly by a disciple of Trotsky called Julian Gorkin and General Leandro Salazar, the man in charge of the criminal investigation following the murder. The second book came out several years later. Its author was a seasoned American journalist and "Russia watcher" since before the Russian Revolution of 1917, Isaac Don Levine. *The Mind of an Assassin* offered a dramatic description of the events that led to the assassination - previous attempts to kill Trotsky undertaken by Mexican Stalinists, the extraordinary security precautions in Trotsky's villa, the tensions and anxieties that ruled the life of its inhabitants who never knew where the next blow would strike. For a time the asssassin's identity was a mystery, and the man himself, "Marcos," as he first called himself, refused to give any information; Levine's was the first of the books on this subject to identify the murderer, Roman Mercader, as a Spanish Communist and GPU agent.

I read the books with bated breath. Levine's especially was far and away more suspenseful than any spy thrillers I ever read, including the novels of Eric Ambler, which I discovered at that time. (It was at Don Levine's farm in southern Maryland, a few years later, that I met an astonishing figure from the past - Alexander Kerensky, head of the short-lived Provisional Government that took power after the Tsar's abdication in February 1917. I remember a handsome old man, walking in the garden, arm-in-arm with a young man whom he regaled with the story of how he was tricked and defeated by Vladimir Ilyich Lenin and Lev Davidovich Trotsky, a story which he apparently never tired of telling.)

But the last stage of my Trotsky saga concerned Max Shachtman himself. I recall vividly the first time I saw him. Shachtman was then in his early fifties, with a gleaming cranium and a rather rasping and powerful voice. His group invited Earl Browder, former Secretary of the American CP, to a debate on the crucial question of the day - namely, "Is the Soviet Union a Socialist State?" Browder had only recently been expelled from the American Communist party, where his Moscow-approved line of reasonable cooperation with the capitalist powers now clashed with the new "left-wing" turn of international communism, also, of course, ordered by Moscow.

Browder accepted the invitation, and I was amazed when I saw him enter the poorly lit Manhattan Hall in the lower East Side accompanied by a dozen or so of his followers, distributing Browder's latest tracts. The auditorium was packed, mostly by opponents of Browder, by no means all of them Trotskyites. Everyone was visibly tense. What was happening now in an obscure auditorium in lower Manhattan seemed vastly more important than the Korean War, or the McCarthy furor, or the debacle of US policy in China. "Is the Soviet Union a Socialist state?" was the issue of the hour, or more to the point - who, Shachtman or Browder, would claim victory in the bout between the forces of darkness and light?

First Browder and then Shachtman outlined their positions, well-known to the enormous, rapt audience. Towards the end of the latter's oration Shachtman, a brilliant public speaker, began to recite the names of once illustrious Communist leaders who were executed by Stalin's henchmen in Moscow, Bucharest, Budapest, Prague and Sofia. Then he pointed a finger straight at Browder and exclaimed: "There - but for an accident of geography - stands a corpse!"

The audience went wild. After the tumult subsided, Browder went up to the microphone and bellowed: "This is the last time I shall ever appear on the same podium with a defender of American imperialism!" and turned towards the exit. The audience broke into laughter: Shachtman had, after all, just concluded a spirited attack on American imperialism and the Korean War. It was a superb ending to the most dramatic public debate I ever experienced.

In Irving Howe's autobiography, *A Margin of Hope*, he describes this historic event. Not only was Howe present, he was in fact the inspirer of Shachtman's *coup de grace*: "We sat in our dingy Fourteenth Street Headquarters discussing what Shachtman should say in the debate," he wrote. "Treat Browder, I said, as if he were an East European communist leader slated for show-trial and purge. Shachtman grinned." I told Howe of the excitement that came over me when I read that passage in his book. "I was there," I said excitedly, "I heard it. I saw it!" Howe grinned.

In the next few years, my preoccupation with Trotsky waned, though it never entirely disappeared: in 1993 I read with fascination Anita Burdman Heserman's *Politics, Logic and Love*, a thoroughly absorbing biography of Jean van Heijenoort, one of Trotsky's most dedicated secretaries, who later became one of the world's leading mathematical logicians. Trotskyite literature about Russia, so indispensable at first, grew largely superfluous in view of the growing number of bona fide scholarly books being published. And the lusty battles within the America Left became increasingly irrelevant as the Left as a whole ceased to play much of a role in American political and intellectual life. In time, sectarian disputes were superseded by the rise of divergent Sovietological schools of thought, and to intellectual altercations no less acidulous than those that had rocked the confined world of American radicals.

In fact, some of the participants in these battles had cut their teeth in the debates on whether the Soviet Union was or was not "a degenerated workers' state," and whether terror had any place in a revolutionary Marxist movement. Their knowledge and polemical skills came in handy as they turned to such questions as whether "totalitarian" was the correct term to describe Soviet society, or who was primarily responsible for the cold war. These impinged on issues far beyond the confines of strictly academic studies, affecting American policy towards the Soviet Union, China, Indochina and Latin America in far-reaching ways.

But one coda remains by way of an adieu to the subject of Lev Davidovich Trotsky. It concerns Max Shachtman. Shortly after his victorious appearance at Manhattan Hall, Shachtman decided to retire temporarily from active participation in American sectarian politics. He did not do it out of disillusionment, nor did he revise his basic views. I think he simply wanted to spend some time thinking and writing, a wish made possible by the University of Wisconsin, which invited him to spend two years as (his term) "Resident American Radical." One major result of this sojourn was his book *The Bureaucratic Revolution - the Rise of the Stalinist State* (1962) - a worthy, if wordy, recapitulation of his major political views, including his criticism of Trotsky.

I met him a few times during this period, once or twice in the house of Alexander Dallin, son of David Dallin and at that time head of the Russian (later Harriman) Institute at Columbia University. I myself was already launched on my Sovietological career - first at Yale University Graduate School, then as an editor for the US Information Agency. And while I was no longer hooked on Trotsky, I was still very eager to meet his most distinguished one-time follower. Shachtman was all I had expected him to be: articulate, witty, inquisitive. But one quality struck me most – one I came to see later on as quite characteristic of most American Communist or ex-Communist leaders I met. Shachtman was astonishingly provincial. Obviously well read in all the Marxist and anti-Marxist classics, with a solid knowledge of contemporary history, and a shrewd understanding of human frailties - especially those of his political opponents - he nevertheless lacked the sweep of a true intellectual. He seemed hardly interested in literature, art - anything, in fact, outside the ken of partisan politics.

Even his sense of humor, I noticed, was circumscribed. He thought it was very amusing to claim that he did "not write articles or essays, only theses." His most scathing epithet was "Menshevik," a word meant to denote cowardice, weakness, duplicity, fawning. It was a carryover from his days as an orthodox Leninist, but it sounded strange coming from a man who himself had become in effect (without admitting it) a Menshevik - that is, a moderate socialist.

In 1956, the American Socialist Party admitted Shachtman and the remnant of his Independent Socialist League, on condition that they would not form a faction within the party. In fact, within a year there was a distinct "pro-Shachtman" faction as well as an "anti-Shachtman" faction within the Socialist Party, both drawn from the ranks of the previous members of the Independent Socialist League. How the miniscule SP, once the proud home of Eugene V. Debs and Norman Thomas, could accommodate so much factionalism was something of a mystery. But perhaps it wasn't. The party soon folded. And Max Shachtman died in 1972. Since he considered himself, until the very end, a "true" Bolshevik, it could be said, in the immortal words of Bertram Wolfe, that he died that most unnatural death of an old Bolshevik - a natural death.

12

Into Sovietology

*The approaching future. Jewish non-Jews. Soviet studies.
Hot war, cold war. Kak skazat' po-russki. Coded messages.
Conventional Courses. Bertram D. Wolfe. My career begins.*

As my tenure at CCNY drew to an end, I began to feel an ever-more-pressing need to make a decision about my future. Unlike most of my fellow students, I did not enter college with a clear notion of what I wanted to do with my life. A good number of them had, already in high school or as freshmen in college, fixed their minds on law, medicine, teaching, engineering. I did not envy them, though my parents would question me anxiously about my plans. I wanted, I told them petulantly, to take "interesting" courses in college, whatever their formal field might be. I felt I had enough time to choose a definite profession, that I wanted to defer the choice as long as I could, with its corollary limitations and obligatory courses on subjects of little concern to me. (Why on earth, I argued with my academic advisor, should I take one course in physics and one in chemistry, neither of which interested me in the slightest? He finally relented, allowing me to take only one of these two courses.)

Yet as time went on, a certain pattern in my academic life began to emerge. By virtue of my childhood and teen-age experiences, as well as of my ideological upbringing, I was smitten - as this narrative plainly demonstrates - by several rather bulky issues, all of them interrelated - Russia, socialism, communism, and the Jewish conundrum, which with all its religious and political fissures impinged on a larger, multifarious world. What student of modern history would not eventually confront the perplexing question of Jewish involvement in radical political movements, why so many Jews flocked to radical parties that promised deliverance from general social and economic evils as well as from national and religious oppression? First by chance but gradually more deliberately, I began to gravitate towards courses relating to my areas of interest. I elected a course on Russian History, two courses on 19th and 20th century political thought, one on nationalism. In addition, I wrote papers specifically related to those areas of interest, thus my paper on Prokofiev, and another, for an art course, on Soviet socialist realism, the theory that, in the apt words of one critic, Louis Fischer, required art to "treat the present as though it did not exist and the future as if it had already arrived."[5]

By the mid-1940s politics and academic scholarship in the United States converged, at least in some respects. A welcome development for me personally, it allowed me to join a specific discipline while still remaining a "generalist," something I had desperately been yearning for. By convergence I have in mind the increased interest in and preoccupation with the Soviet Union, which in turn generated an increase in courses on the Russian language, literature, history and government. Such courses had been part of the curricula in many universities, but not coherently, and without impinging in one way or another on U.S. policies or American public opinion. From 1941 on, when Russia joined the war, until about a year after the end of hostilities, cordiality and cooperation, albeit laced by a hefty amount of wariness, marked U.S.-Soviet relations: yesterday's adversary suddenly became an ally, a situation not easy to accept, especially by those with strong anti-Communist views.

But this did not last long. In 1946 came the Cold War, and with it a growing atmosphere of suspicion and war psychosis, resulting in a feverish obsession with the construction of air raid shelters - as if no

American home could be safe without one; compulsory air raid tests in schools and universities; the strident concern about the "threat" of communism, a mirror-image - albeit a greatly distorted one - of Stalinist paranoia about internal enemies. These developments, well known but worth recapitulating, did not occur overnight, but incrementally, and their cumulative impact was enormous.

This change in the political climate radically affected Russian studies. For a long time, the scholar interested in the history of Russia, or its literature, or, say, 19th century political opposition in Russia, had been relatively isolated, cultivating his or her ideas, maintaining professional ties only with other individual scholars. There was no community of Russian scholars, nor any systematic support either from academic foundations or from the government. There were certainly a number of prominent historians, legal scholars, literary specialists and economists, such as Geroid Robinson, John Hazard, George Kennan, Bernard Pares, Gleb Struve and Abram Bergson, among others, and a fair number of lesser lights, too. People with personal experience in the Soviet Union and/or political opponents constituted a separate category of specialists, some of the best in the field: they brought to the subject their own partisan political views and passions but often provided exceptionally well-informed analysis and outstanding insights.

The Trotskyites produced no scholars of distinction comparable to Nicolaevsky or Schwartz, but their journals contained much reliable information for budding Soviet scholars like myself, in addition to considerable news about the activities of the numerically-small if highly vocal movement. *The New Leader*, social democratic in its orientation, occupied a unique position among left-wing American weeklies. Unlike *The New Republic* and *The Nation*, both given to flirting with quasi-Communist and fellow-traveling notions, *The New Leader* maintained its staunch democratic position. For Frieda Kirchway, long-time editor of *The Nation*, criticism of the Soviet Union was a species of benighted American ignorance if not indeed outright fascism. Not so Sol Levitas, first editor of *The New Leader*, who published thoughtful articles on the Soviet Union and on Communist and socialist parties throughout the world. (Later the journal came out every fortnight and then every two months, surviving until 2006.)

Levitas, an erstwhile Menshevik, spoke English with a heavy Russian accent and expected all good social democrats to contribute to his journal. Among his singular claims to fame was that in 1918 he had been elected for one day as Chairman of the Workers' and Sailors' Soviet - in effect, mayor - of Vladivostok. After he came to the United States in the late 1920s, he successfully parlayed his cachet into pressure on various comrades to contribute to his magazine. Gratis.

Slowly but gradually, I began contributing short pieces to *The New Leader*. Far more experienced writers than myself received but a pittance to write for *The New Leader*: they did it out of loyalty rather than professional commitment... Once, however, I published a piece in *The New Republic*, and Levitas called me on the phone immediately, to inquire about the reason for my apostasy. "But Sol," I said, "*The New Republic* pays for its articles, and you do not." There was a moment of silence, and then came Levitas' gruff heavily-accented voice: " But Abe," he said, "remember your roots!" I was speechless.

After the war the situation materially altered. At first slowly, then more swiftly, Russia ceased being a subject of purely academic interest, even within the academy. Columbia University and Harvard founded institutions - the Russian Institute and the Russian Research Center respectively - devoted to the study of the Soviet Union and Communist-ruled countries of Eastern Europe, gathering scholars trained in different disciplines but united in their interest in specific geographic areas. Other universities – Indiana, Illinois, Michigan, Wisconsin, California – followed suit. Thus Soviet studies found a home – or several homes – and attained academic legitimacy. Foundations began to advance money for individual and institutional research; so did the U.S. government.

Some government agencies favored scholars with a bent for anti-Communist crusades and some U.S. intelligence agencies established "dummy" foundations whose well-paid staff produced exposés of Communist "infiltration" in educational institutions, Soviet espionage activities and the like. On the whole, though, the money came with no strings attached. I suppose both private foundations and federal institutions came to grasp the value of independent scholarship, whether or not it fitted in with the "cold war" atmosphere of those days. As a result, students with particular scholarly (and also political) interest in the Soviet Union and Eastern Europe flocked to the mushrooming "area studies" centers. Harvard received a large grant from the Department of Defense to organize and analyze extensive interviews with some of the thousands of Soviet émigrés who found themselves in Germany and other European countries after the war. Other universities found sponsors for large-scale studies as well. Thus a new discipline came into being: Sovietology. (Eventually similar Far Eastern institutes also began to flourish.)

Here I saw my chance. In 1949 I applied to the Russian Institute at Columbia University; I was rejected. Since Columbia required students to take two degrees simultaneously (sociology, for instance, in addition to Soviet Studies), I was not too disheartened. Harvard had similar requirements. Yale did not, so I applied and, to my delight, was accepted. Yale had liberal requirements: only one course, on the Soviet Communist Party, taught by a Rand Corporation scholar, Nathan Leites, was obligatory, and it sounded enthralling. Moreover, Yale offered very intensive Russian language study, which greatly appealed to me. Yale was not cheap, even then, but the GI Bill would cover fees otherwise prohibitive for my family. A brief meeting with a few Yale faculty members convinced me: Yale, I decided, was for me. I became restless, impatient to bid good-bye to City College and to embark upon my new academic – and hopefully professional – career.

And so in late September 1950, brimming with hope and expectation, I enrolled as a graduate student at Yale University. A comfortable room at the Yale Graduate Center, with windows looking out onto the courtyard, made me feel instantaneously at home. In addition to residential rooms, the Graduate Center housed classrooms and a dining room: it became my universe. The Graduate School had just begun admitting women, and when a woman student entered the dining room, every man seated at the table would stand up as a mark of respect – rather a far cry from the manners (such as they were) that prevailed at City College. The large washrooms were but a few feet away from my room. One regular morning visitor attracted my attention: a German in his early 20s, tall and gaunt, whose name was – truly – Karl Hochschwanger

("Highpregnant"). Hochschwanger would enter the bathroom in the morning, fully dressed, then remove his jacket, roll up his shirtsleeves a precise three inches, loosen (but never take off!) his tie and proceed to shave and brush his teeth. Ablutions completed, he would roll down his sleeves, tighten his tie, put on his jacket and depart, leaving behind him a strong odor of eau de cologne. I watched him through the corner of my eye, mesmerized.

Three courses formed the backbone of my studies at Yale, of which the first was Russian language. Russian was of course familiar to my ears. Many of my relatives spoke Russian, including my father, and I had heard it often, especially after the Soviets occupied Lithuania. (We'd even been taught Russian for a few months in Vilna, though I can't say I learned much.) I had a certain advantage over my fellow-students as they struggled mightily to distinguish between hard and soft consonants, dentalized "d" and non-dentalized "t." My Polish also proved useful. The course consisted of daily three-hour sessions, from 9 am to noon. A Russian speaker - a "native informant" - who was not allowed to say a word in English ran each session, and once a week we met with Professor William Stuart Cornyn, to study grammar and syntax but never oral proficiency, given Dr. Cornyn's notorious pronunciation. The native speakers, with some of whom I later struck up friendships, taught us words, phrases, and idiomatic expressions whose English translations appeared in our textbooks, though we were instructed never to use them in the classroom. With this system we accumulated a fairly large vocabulary in the first few weeks, which we could use with the help of the grammar taught us by Prof. Cornyn. I thought it was an ingenious and effective approach, and soon found I could engage in simple conversations with my informants and fellow-students.

The second course was the brainstorm of Nathan Leites. He had, as far as I know, no previous record of any scholarly accomplishment. But in keeping with the Zeitgeist, Leites formulated a set of principles that he called, and then entitled his book, "The Operational Code of the Politburo." According to Leites, true Bolsheviks behaved according to a set of principles adumbrated in Lenin and Stalin's writings. Hence mastery of these principles was *de rigueur*: study the texts, explain the system. His approach became fashionable in those years and won Rand's support. As he saw it, this "operational code" offered the Soviet party a tested tool in political conduct vis-à-vis other parties and in Soviet foreign policy. And for Western analysts, this "operational code" had predictive value, providing a blueprint according to which one could always (or almost always) anticipate from the Communists certain behavior in given situations. It was thus a device useful both to the Communists and to us, their analysts and/or antagonists.

One might think that serious scholars would dismiss as absurd the notion of any such "code" - which in Leites' class we had to learn by rote, much like the Chinese were expected to know by heart Mao's "Little Red Book." Oddly enough, they did not, for his slim volume had the virtues of so many holy writs: clear and unwavering rules, rooted in history, sanctified by its "scientific" character (which its disciples took for granted), and moreover validated by actual experience, as illustrated by specific examples at the end of each chapter. Thus, in the chapter entitled "Deception:" "Bolshevik doctrine stresses the use of deception as an enemy device and the danger of not perceiving this. In 1926 Stalin stated: *Lenin often said that it is difficult to take revolutionaries by the use of a rough fist, but that sometimes it is very easy to take them by kindness. We must never forget this truth...* Hence a high degree of political insight includes a high degree of suspiciousness... In 1926, Stalin said: *To deceive our party is not such an easy matter.*"[6] This highly sophisticated analysis came fifteen years after the Terror of the 1930s, when thousands of Communists were sent to their deaths for presumably letting themselves be deceived by the "Enemy," disguised as Trotskyites, British spies, "Zinovievites," etc.

In another passage, from "The Control of Feelings," Leites notes gravely that the "Party line must be rationally calculated and must be distinguished from 'moods'." He then cites Lenin's analysis of the Menshevik rejection of boycott of the new Russian parliament in 1905: *The Mensheviks were wrong not because they showed in this question a lack of revolutionary mood but because...[they] remained behind the objectively revolutionary situation. It is easy to confuse these causes of the error of the Mensheviks, but it is inappropriate for a Marxist to do so.* (20) More than half a century on, the notion that only Bolsheviks were aware that yielding to emotions was incompatible with political decision-making seems quite preposterous. To cite an obscure historical incident as validating this interpretation seems even more preposterous. Yet in the early 1950s this and similar formulations seemed - at least to some students of the Soviet Union - to express essential truths about Bolshevik thought and behavior. Why? The only explanation I can find is, again, the *Zeitgeist*, through whose lens a Communist - whether perceived sympathetically, antagonistically, or "objectively"- became a unique political animal, different from animals of other political stripes and beliefs. To define, "quantify," and codify these traits became a legitimate branch of scholarship.

In fact, I myself was very much taken with the mystifications of Leites' "code," and even if I had some misgivings (which we could discuss freely in the classroom), I was happy to take the course. I read much interesting material, including Bertram D. Wolfe's magnificent biography of Lenin, Trotsky and Stalin up to 1917, *Three Who Made a Revolution*, and the classroom discussions were lively and entertaining.

Two years on, after I had left Yale, Leites came out with another book that further developed his theories. Called *A Study of Bolshevism*, it contended that the "operational code" actually derived from many of the writings of 19th century Russian authors. Leites cited at length from Dostoyevsky, Tolstoy, Turgenev and the like, selecting some passages that presumably served the Bolsheviks as guides to action, and others that presented negative examples, ideas to resist as incompatible with Bolshevik values. Again, despite the patent absurdity of reading 19th century fiction as political manuals, Leites' book earned a good deal of serious scholarly cachet. So did his *The Ritual of Liquidation*, published a year later, which ostensibly proved that the both the defendants in the notorious Moscow Trials of the 1930s and their prosecutor, Andrei Vishinsky, were acting out patterns of Bolshevik norms and beliefs, above all demonstrating their loyalty to the party even at the price of one's death (a sad result "subjectively," but "objectively" necessary).

The book was a gloss of Arthur Koestler's version of the Moscow Trials in his *Darkness at Noon*, as well as of a few other books of the 1950s that dealt with the Soviet purges. Superficially logical, devastatingly persuasive, they nonetheless represented a species of mystification. The idea that Rykov, Bukharin, Zinoviev, all venerable Bolsheviks, were persuaded to confess to, for instance, planning the assassination of Stalin, as their last service to the Party may be dramatically gripping, but it is balderdash. We now know definitely what plenty of us suspected at the time: that many arrested Communists were shot *in camera* after secret *pro forma* trials, or sometimes no trials at all, and that most of those who confessed did so to save their families from arrest and death (the promises to spare the families were as sham as the trials), often after weeks or months of physical and psychological torture. In fact Nikolai Yezhov, the macabre head of the NKVD at the height of the purges, is said by one historian (Simon Sebag Montefiore, in his *Stalin: The Court of the Red Tsar*) to have routinely come to Politburo meetings in a blood-spattered jacket.

Leites was not unique in his pseudo-scholarship. Another popular theory, advanced by Geoffrey Gorer, a British anthropologist, attributed responsibility for the Russians' supposed propensity for authoritarianism and obedience to tight swaddling of infants. The American anthropologist Margaret Mead fully approved of this theory. So did others, though plenty of Soviet scholars considered it rubbish. Even then, however, these theories did not constitute the core of Soviet studies. I took a course in Russian history with the esteemed Russian historian George Vernadsky, who came to the United States in the late 1920s; his lectures consistently mainly of material in the chapter of his book he had assigned to us last time we met. Still, one could learn much from him.

Soviet politics at Yale was taught by Frederick Barghoorn, Cultural Attaché at the US Embassy in Moscow in the 1940s. Barghoorn filled his solid if not brilliant lectures with valuable information and intelligent insight, based on his personal observations and experience, and I benefited from them far more than from Leites' occasional flashes of luminosity. Barghoorn was an enormously decent, man, quiet and retiring. Until his late sixties, he lived with his mother in New Haven, and her death, he confided in me (to my astonishment), shocked him to the core: the apartment, a few streets away from the Graduate Center, suddenly became cold and lonely.

Despite my willing participation in political activities at City College, I found the quiet scholarly atmosphere at Yale much to my liking. I could spend hours at my desk in Sterling Library, on the eighth floor, overlooking the campus. I marveled at the bounty of its open stacks. And I would always find books or brochures I had heard nothing about, which whetted my intellectual appetite. The history of late 19th century Russia held me in thrall. I could not tear myself away form Alexander Herzen's autobiography *Past and Thoughts*, from books dealing with the People's Will movement, the anarchist movement, and the like.

Social life at Yale was not terribly exciting. I befriended a few graduate students, including Alexander Shenker, who stayed on at Yale teaching in the Department of Slavic Languages and Literature, and occasionally a small group of us would descend upon a Greek dive downtown for a sumptuous meal at virtually no cost. After a while we realized that the dive served as the headquarters of local Near Eastern call girls. They were not particularly pretty, but lively, and loved dancing to bazouki music. We ogled the food the owner cooked for us more hungrily than the girls. It was inevitably lamb and rice pilaf, delicious and plentiful. The owner, a formidable man, also made some ouzo on the sly, and treated us all to a glass apiece. "Myself," he would say, "I don't drink much of this stuff – perhaps just a glass once every two hours."

Female companionship of the respectable type was hard to find in New Haven, unless you were willing to go to parties with undergraduates and generally participate in their pastimes (bars, football games and such), not my cup of tea. I had a girl friend in New York, and most weekends I would take the train or hitch a ride with my friend Shenker and stay there a day or two. Altogether, then, life in New Haven was quite agreeable.

In the summer of 1952, with one more year at Yale ahead of me, my good friend Uriel Weinreich relayed an offer to spend the summer working on Soviet materials for an outfit called "U.S. Government Press Bureau," shortly to be incorporated into the U.S. Information Agency. I was one of five or six students assigned to Bertram Wolfe, who at that time enjoyed the title of "Special Ideological Advisor to the Voice of America," that eventually became the radio broadcasting arm of U.S.I.A. Wolfe had a fascinating personal history, including membership the Mexican CP during World War I and subsequently in the American Communist Party, and a trip with some of his comrades to Moscow, where Stalin lectured him on his criminal ideological deviations: meeting the First Secretary face-to-face was an experience Wolfe would never forget (or stop talking about...) He left the CP in the early 1930s and devoted himself – successfully – to the writing of contemporary history.

When I met him Wolfe wanted to generate papers on the Russian Revolution of 1917 as a means of countering Soviet propaganda that baldly falsified Bolshevik history, converted Stalin into Supreme Leader far before he assumed that mantle, and virtually erased Trotsky's role in the formation of the Soviet state. Anything that demonstrated the mendacity of Soviet official history, reasoned Wolfe, was a good thing - provided, of course, it was accurate and well-researched. I wrote several papers that were later incorporated into Voice of America broadcasts. I also published a revised version of one of them in the professional journal *Russian Review* - my first published work in Sovietology!

Wolfe, a tall man then in his sixties, held himself very erect, and generally treated his charges in a generous, avuncular manner. He was charmingly vain. He once told us how he and his wife stopped in a nondescript motel somewhere in the depths of Oklahoma. As he related it, when the proprietor read his name in the hotel registry, he exclaimed "Could you be the author of *Three Who Made a Revolution*!?" Wolfe admitted as much, and the proprietor, bursting with pride and pleasure, gave the Wolfes the best room in the motel and a meal at the hotel's expense. "I found it hard to decline such a generous offer," Wolfe said, modestly.

In the summer of 1952, then, I became, to all intents and purposes, a bona fide, paid Sovietologist. In the meantime, the U.S. Information Agency, just then being established as a formal government institution, inquired whether I would accept a job as a "Soviet analyst," provided I could receive the necessary security clearance. I found it impossible to turn down such a tempting offer. My career was about to take off.

13

Sovietology *Engagement*

*Birth of a Journal. Scribblers and Gumshoes. What's in a Name?
A Serious Rift. Same or Different? Have Journal Will Travel.
Dramatis Personae. The Social Democratic Option.*

For nearly twenty years, from 1952 through 1970, I edited a bimonthly journal called *Problems of Communism*, sponsored by the United States Information Agency in Washington, D.C. The journal's first decade were the formative years of the rapidly developing new discipline, Sovietology, a term that had not even existed a few years back. Now it became all the rage. In the 1950s, hardly a month passed – or so it seemed to me – without one university or another opening its own "Russian," or "Russian and East European" or "Russian and Far Eastern" institute.

In this climate, the way I became editor of *Problems of Communism* is both absurd and revealing. Drawn by the promise of working in a field close to my heart, I joined the United States Information Agency (USIA) in the summer of 1952, and after a brief stint in New York City moved to Washington. The Agency was headquartered at 1776 Pennsylvania Avenue, a rather nondescript building at the corner of Pennsylvania Ave. and 18th Street, not far from the White

House. I was assigned a small room with a desk, chair, some bookshelves, a typewriter. My instructions were to write brief essays or stories about current events concerning the Soviet Union, or historical events of topical relevance, to be used either by USIA's daily "wireless service" or by the Voice of America (VOA). I was pleased with this broad assignment since I could more or less choose the topic and did not have to navigate the usual bureaucratic shoals and controls.

What could be more pleasing? A less torrid environment, for one thing. Washington was beastly hot, and at that time many government buildings, including mine, had no air conditioning, so we were free to leave around 3 pm if the temperature reached 92 degrees. (Within a year or two, Washington office life was transformed by the installation of air conditioning.) One summer day I was sitting in my room when the door opened, and in came a man whose name I do not remember, whose face is a blur in my memory and who as far as I know never again crossed my path. Looking at me quizzically, he asked in a brusque fashion: "Say, Brumberg, aren't you some kind of a Soviet expert?" I hesitated, then modestly concurred. The man glanced at me and continued, "We are starting a new magazine to be called *Problems of Communism*. It will be distributed through USIA posts in Europe and elsewhere. And you will be in charge of it." This said, he turned around and strode out of the room. I was stunned. What? In charge of a magazine to be distributed throughout the world? Must be some kind of a poor joke.

But it wasn't. Within a few days, I was introduced to a recent graduate of Smith College, Terry Thompson, the woman with whom I was to produce the new publication. An "experimental issue" was already in the works, and issue No. 1 was almost ready, so our job was to complete that issue and then start working on a new one. The journal, whose purpose was to report on and interpret developments in the Communist world, would come out once in two months. It was made clear to us that the magazine must be on a respectable intellectual level, that it should strive for maximum fairness and objectivity, and that it should above all avoid being seen as yet another "propaganda rag." This fully accorded with both Terry

Thompson's and my predilections. So we accepted the assignment with enthusiasm.

Terry turned out to be a splendid editor, and about a year and a half later she was appointed Managing (i.e. Deputy Chief) Editor, and I, Editor-in-Chief. Two new people had in the meantime joined our staff - Clarke Kawakami, a Nisei Harvard-trained historian in his early fifties, and Cary Fisher, considerably younger, son of a Catholic Czech refugee with an academic background in East European affairs. Clarke was the model of a perfect gentleman, kind, averse to displays of emotion, and an inveterate smoker: by the end of the day his ashtray, clean and shining in the morning, would overflow with cigarette stubs. Cary was charming and easy-going. We had much in common and I delighted in conversing with him. The four of us made a good team.

Early on, and much to my dismay, my appointment caused a minor squall. I wrote to Bertram Wolfe, whom I considered my mentor, informing him about my new position, but it turned out that the news did not altogether please him. In a rather peremptory letter to the head of USIA (with a drop copy to me), Wolfe acknowledged that I was "indeed a gifted young man," but he thought it scandalous to saddle me, so "young and inexperienced," with a position of such "enormous political power." Given the present dangerous state in world affairs, wrote Wolfe, and the fragile nature of Soviet-Western relations, circumspection was mandatory; every decision mattered. He did not think my appointment fulfilled these requirements.

"Enormous political power!" What on earth did Wolfe have in mind, I wondered: something along the lines of the rumpus among Russian socialists in the first years of the 20th century, concerning the candidates for editor of the party newspaper *Iskra* (Spark), Lenin and his more "dovish" adversaries? Lenin's eventual victory did indeed have some important consequences, including a split between the Bolsheviks and the more moderate Mensheviks. Could Wolfe possibly be comparing the role of *Iskra* then with the (potential) role of *POC* now? It sounded preposterous, but given Wolfe's passionate preoccupation with Russian history and historical parallels, perhaps not implausible.

In any event, the head of USIA responded by assuring Wolfe that he "knew Abe Brumberg as an exceptionally capable man" (we had never met), an opinion all his associates shared (?), and he was certain that Wolfe would eventually come to accept his choice. About a year and a half later, he did. He had made a mistake, wrote Wolfe to me. And he was delighted to admit he had been wrong. I was still young and hardly bursting with self-confidence: Wolfe's missive touched me profoundly.

Our staff being, by ordinary bureaucratic standards, miniscule, and our work virtually unrelated to any other USIA activities, we found ourselves effectively isolated from the rest of the Agency, with the possible exception of a few people in VOA who worked on the Russian, Polish, Hungarian, Ukrainian and other politically-related "desks." We had more contact with some people in the State Department, especially in its Research Division, than in the Information Agency. Nathan Glick, who edited *America*, another USIA-sponsored "intellectual" journal, became a friend. Glick was particularly fond of recollecting his days at C.C.N.Y. in the 1930s, where for a time he was a member of a Trotskyite group. Once he thought he found somebody even mildly interested in the subject, he would regale him or her with a meticulous account of his political maturation, and a disquisition on the nature of Trotskyism in general.

The fact that I had only limited intellectual and social contacts in USIA did not bother me. I had, to tell the truth, little respect for the motley group of journalists and bureaucrats working there. Many of them knew quite a bit about U.S. history, institutions and current events, but most knew astonishingly little about the outside world. I remember an editor of *America* once calling me to make sure of the accuracy of a translation from Russian that he – knowing no Russian - was editing. "I noticed," he said with some embarrassment, "that the English version is considerably shorter than the Russian version, which made me wonder whether some of my translators [mostly former Soviet citizens] were trying to pull a fast one on me - you never know about those Russians, do you?" I read both texts, and assured him the translations were fine: word counts vary, after all, and Russian uses more of them than English. He was vastly relieved.

As for the "security personnel," more or less amiable rednecks, the less contact between them and myself, the better I felt. Their job was to investigate the background of anyone to be employed by the Agency, such as potential contributors to *Problems of Communism*, to determine whether he or she could be regarded as a "security risk." "One-time" use was granted automatically, but if you planned to employ the person more often, a security clearance was mandatory. It was an obnoxious job, open, of course, to all sorts of calumny, politically or personally inspired.

Every encounter with these gumshoes (all with FBI credentials, I was sure) made my blood run cold. On only two occasions did the head of security graciously allow me to see the "security file" of a *POC* contributor: I remember one as being a jumble of gossip dressed up as a supposedly reliable account of a pointedly "anti-American" talk delivered at some meeting by the person under investigation. In general, the two most common charges were "political disloyalty" and sexual deviance, usually homosexuality. It was hard to tell which of the two posed – to official eyes - more of a threat to the foundations of the Republic.

For the top bureaucrats who were supposed to make the ultimate decisions, distinctions were of little concern: the person either was or was not a potential embarrassment, someone who might be singled out by a Congressman anxious to settle a personal account with the Agency or wedded to an especially obnoxious political agenda. The mentality that had facilitated the rise of McCarthyism was still in the air. I was glad that *POC* was considered small potatoes, below the radar screen of politicians, though secretly I fantasized about a clash between the politicians and myself, full of fire and brimstone... Luckily, *POC* remained in the shadows, preoccupied with the continual internal tremors and crises of Communist countries and Communist parties throughout he world.

In the early 1950s, when I came to Washington, the city was still very much part of the Old South, and distinctly provincial, despite its federal buildings and the government's international ties. Public transportation had just been desegregated, but "Colored Only" signs still disfigured the walls of gas and bus stations. Many blacks, out of long habit, moved to the back of a bus or streetcar, leaving the front seats to whites. Schooling was still segregated, as were all commercial restaurants and hotels. Only on the property of the federal government – cafeterias in the Departments of State and Labor, or the National Gallery of the Arts, for instance – could blacks and whites take their meals together.

Naturally, I despised this situation. Discrimination and contempt for "the other" were phenomena I knew well enough. I felt stifled to live in a city where discrimination against members of a specific race was not only generally accepted but implemented and protected by law; I abhorred the hypocrisy of this bigotry vividly on display in the capital of the "most free" and "most democratic" nation on earth, as the official rhetoric insisted. At a corner drug store not far from where I lived, the staff consisted exclusively of blacks; they always served black customers first and whites later, no matter who had come in first. I noted this quiet defiance with grim satisfaction. As the years passed Washington changed from a sleepy Jim Crow town into a cosmopolitan, diverse city, with a much more heterogeneous population and cultural scene.

My own political opinions remained pretty much the same. The Kennedy years provided the single period when I was actually pleased to work for the government, but even those years and to a much greater extent the Johnson years were marred by the Vietnam War. As it evolved as a discipline Sovietology split into different schools, factions, and tendencies. During the years that I edited *Problems of Communism*, the journal generally articulated what I would call the "social democratic" option, a legacy to which I was heir and which resonated among most of my contributors, implicitly or explicitly. In that view, communism, in its Leninist and then Stalinist and Maoist varieties, represented a violent distortion and corruption of an ideology that (like so many utopias) promised Heaven on Earth, delivering instead a monstrous panoply of controls and repression, in many ways worse than what had preceded it. But this system had to be studied, its variant forms analyzed and compared with one another and not simply anathematized, as was much too often the case. The "social democratic" cast of mind fit my contributors and colleagues even though hardly any of them was politically a social democrat (or "democratic socialist"). But I found their views on the Soviet Union and on communism congenial, roughly parallel to those that I had imbibed as a child and in many ways still retained as an adult.

One group of Sovietologists in effect denied that the Soviet Union could ever abandon its totalitarian "essence," nor could other regimes modeled on the Soviet Union. The other maintained that the Soviet Union and its epigones could in time evolve, if not into a democracy (as the Polish-British writer, Isaac Deutscher, believed, for good measure inserting "social" in front of "democracy"), then at least into a more liberal and humane society. While the contributors to *POC* by no means constituted an ideologically monolithic group, they did, by and large, belong to the second, "evolutionary" camp: most of our contributors believed that the Soviet Union and all Communist states were changing, often in a positive direction though too slowly and with much room for improvement. Stalin's death in 1953 – almost as momentous an event for Sovietologists as for Soviet and East Bloc residents - led us to scrutinize for changes specific policies of Communist regimes on censorship, agricultural controls, trade unions. And indeed, changes there were - but what did they amount to? None of us knew, of course. Naturally, there was disagreement within the ranks and within the readership - which made our journal more and more lively.

I recall a somewhat outré essay in one of our symposiums, in which the historian Arthur Schlesinger – admittedly no authority on the Soviet Union - speculated on the possibility of the U.S.S.R. metamorphosing into some kind of one-party pluralistic system, similar to Mexico's Institutional Revolutionary Party, with the communist party retaining power while other groups were given access to the political process. The analogy may have been problematic, but it illustrated the flexibility of the "evolutionary" approach, far more open to daring assumptions than the "totalitarian model," with its rigid rejection of any possible deviation from the centralized political system established by Lenin and then deftly "improved" by Joseph Stalin.

In 1960 we published a symposium entitled "Towards a Communist Welfare State?" Could the Soviet Union, we asked, conceivably develop into an authoritarian one-party state capable of making liberal concessions on wages, work conditions, and the autonomy of professional unions, until that time "transmission belts" entirely subjected to the control of the state? A former colleague of mine at Yale University wrote in: we were "mad" to think Communist regimes could possibly change.

These theories and variations on them resonated in articles written for us by a host of renowned scholars and writers: Merle Fainsod and Adam Ulam of Harvard; Zbigniew Brzezinski, Seweryn Bialer and Alexander Erlich, of Columbia; Hugh Seton-Watson, Peter Wiles and Jane Degras, from London. In 1954, the Swiss journalist and author of a well-known book on Tito, Ernst Halperin, exploded a bombshell in our pages by firmly predicting that the Soviet Union was about to install "workers' councils" on the Yugoslav model. Whether Yugoslav workers' councils were as "democratic" as the Yugoslavs claimed they were another matter but Halperin thought so, and provoked a storm of responses.

A dramatic example of the differences between the two camps, evolutionist and (for want of a better word) totalitarian, and of their impact on international relations concerned the Sino-Soviet relationship. Once ideologically glued to each other, despite their different origins and political histories, the two regimes were often assumed to be practically identical, and bound by insoluble ties. ("Moscow and Peking Are Brothers," sang the Red Army Chorus – as no doubt did its counterpart in China.) In the early 1960s, however, "evolutionist" scholars assiduously following the Soviet and Chinese press, as well as the behavior of the two protagonists, concluded that a rift was developing between them, one that could lead to a complete ideological and diplomatic breakdown. The "totalitarians" violently disagreed, deeming the rift a bluff designed by both Communist powers to hoodwink the West. The fire-breathing articles on both sides, they said, were all cunning fabrications.

CIA analysts joined the dispute, themselves dividing into two contending groups, each sporting its own in-house publication, both tolerated by the CIA. To this day I cannot explain how such freedom of the press could be tolerated within the bowels of the Central Intelligence Agency: perhaps agency directors simply overlooked it, perhaps it was made possible by the chasm that separated the research department of CIA from what we often referred to as "the department of the dirty tricks," perhaps it was an impressive tribute to basic American democratic values. Whichever, it remained a conundrum, and it didn't last long.

We found out that the main spokesman of the "pro-rift" faction was a young academic by the name of Donald Zagoria. I asked him whether he could give us an article on this subject, he agreed, and amazingly enough, the bosses of the Agency, who had to approve every single article published outside by one of their officers, sanctioned it. We read, liked, and ran it. (Zagoria, incidentally, left the Agency to take up an academic position in a university.) Thus the pages of *POC* became even more a battleground for passionate polemics, with the supporters of the rift theory clearly in a majority. In time, the Soviet Union and China fell out with each other openly, and the proponents of "bluff" theory had to retire.

Of course dissimulation remained part of the Communist *modus operandi*. An outstanding case in point was labeling the East European regimes "people's democracies," so as to distinguish them presumably from classic Marxist-Leninist states. Thus Poland and East Germany for instance, both claimed to be multi-party systems, though the political groups in those countries were at best shabby survivals of genuine pre-war political parties, and all took orders from and swore fealty to "the leading role" of the CP.

In 1961, during one of my first post-war trips to Poland, I went to see the head of the "Democratic Party" (*Stronnictwo Demokratyczne*), Leon Chajn, in an office lined with the collected works of Lenin and Stalin. The Democratic Party was an offshoot of a liberal middle-class group founded in 1938, fiercely opposed to the nationalistic and violently anti-Semitic National Democrats (*Endecja*) but with no political clout whatsoever. A suave man, Chajn tried to explain to me the dialectical differences between his party and the CP (whose leadership he energetically affirmed), but as I happened to know that he was a pre-war Communist apparatchik assigned to this job in 1949 by the party's Central Committee, our meeting was rather a farce – though a useful one...

Problems of Communism, unlike some other journals in the US and elsewhere, did not claim to be apolitical. It struck an unabashedly political note from the very start. But we tried to be fair. I still remember the terse characterization of it in 1955 by a British scholar in the London *Times*: "ruthless but just." I was delighted: the phrase captured precisely what my colleagues and I were trying to accomplish. Yet could a journal sponsored by a government with an explicitly anti-Communist agenda avoid being a propaganda organ? This was a problem, and indeed a number of people to whom we turned for contributions curtly turned us down as disingenuous. I tried to allay legitimate concerns by adamantly excluding articles that would, by their very subject matter, involve discussions - or rationalizations - of US policy, however subtle. Admittedly, boundaries blurred, but we made every effort to abide by that rule, and so gradually more and more people came to consider us a legitimate forum for various points of view. Pro-US propaganda had no place in our journal.

We were greatly aided by two factors: first, the journal was not subject to any official censorship. Final decisions rested with the editors. Second, our bureaucratic bosses were - not to put too fine a point on it - pathetically ignorant. They did not know much, and they didn't want to know more. As far as they were concerned, *POC* was a handy tool against the "Commies", overly intellectual maybe but in safely anti-Communist hands, so why bother to read it? The head of the Press Service, to which *POC* belonged, was a conservative Republican from Texas, who referred to the Chinese as "Chinamen" and was incautious enough on a few occasions to make disguised anti-Semitic remarks. But he was generally careful (and didn't speak much anyway), so it was difficult to nail him down on his odious views. One of our section's first chiefs was a man by the name of Joseph Dineen, who had taught English literature in a rather obscure Catholic college, and had written a book on Hilaire Belloc. Upon being introduced to the staff, Dineen told us that he felt delightfully at home, having read Marx and Engels "though not in the original Russian." With such supervisors, we decided, we needn't lose sleep about censorship.

The only time I sensed danger was during a contretemps with Strauss-Hupé, a man who would be branded a neo-conservative in later years but who in the 1960s was considered an extreme, perhaps slightly potty, right-winger. Strauss-Hupé, a professor at Pennsylvania State University, co-authored with Stephen Possony, originally from Hungary, and two minor American political scientists a book called *Protracted Conflict*. Their thesis was that every international crisis, however small, was orchestrated by a powerful Communist conspiracy headquartered in Moscow. Vigilance, eternal vigilance against all Communists and their fellow-travelers was therefore essential. I asked historian Alfred Meyer, of Michigan University, to review the book, and he demolished Strauss-Hupé's oeuvre as one of those obsessional anti-Communist works that were beginning to appear in the States like mushrooms after a rain, and with about as much scholarly value. In reply, Strauss-Hupé wrote a screed of about 10,000 words, expressing his and his colleagues' shock at finding a "pro-Communist tract" in the pages of a respectable US Government publication. Unless we retracted it immediately and published his own letter, he would inform Vice President Nixon, Senator John Knowland of California - a man with unblemished anti-Communist credentials - and a few other like-minded personalities of this scandalous event.

For a while, I had a vision of an anti-Communist vendetta, complete with Congressional hearings, directed at my colleagues and myself, possibly resulting in the demise of our journal. (The McCarthy hearings were still fresh in everybody's memory.) Nevertheless, I wrote a curt (too curt, in the opinion of my fellow-editors) letter informing Strauss-Hupé that surely Vice President Nixon and Senator Knowland would be the first to acknowledge Professor Meyer's impeccable credentials as an authority on communism and therefore entitled to review as he chose. We had, I said, no intention of retracting Meyer's piece but would be glad to publish a letter by Strauss-Hupé, of no more than 800 words (300 more than our standard maximum). Lo and behold, Strauss-Hupé responded courteously, taking issue with Meyer, but leaving out the wild-eyed complaints of his original missive. Meyer wrote a brief reply, and we declared the discussion of *Protracted Conflict* at an end. Ten years later, when I happened to run into Strauss-Hupé in Brussels, where he was serving as US Ambassador, he greeted me warmly and neither of us said a word about our on-time tiff.

As the editor of an expanding journal, one of my chief chores (and pleasures) was to locate new contributors and new contributions. Washington offered slim pickings, so fact-finding missions to universities and area-studies centers both in and outside the United States, as well as meetings with journalists who covered our subjects, became virtually mandatory. The more we attracted contributors of excellence (and of eminence), the greater the journal's prestige. Thus, too, my own circle of acquaintances significantly expanded.

The Russian Research Center at Harvard University, located in an old atmospheric building full of unexpected corners and crannies, came to serve as an ideal recruiting ground. One of my first "finds" was Joseph Berliner, a superb economist, then in his late thirties, a warm and generous man, who wrote lucidly and – despite the inherent dryness of his subject – with humor. He contributed one of the best articles to our journal, called "*Blat* Is Higher than Stalin!" – *blat* being slang for "string-pulling" and other semi-legal activities which factory managers depended on if they were to fill their production quotas. The central figure in such transactions was the *tolkach* (roughly, "fixer"). Indeed, without the ubiquity of *blat*, the Soviet Union literally could not have functioned.

Years later, Berliner came to me, visibly worried. It turned out that a colleague, a Soviet émigré, showed him an article "full," Berliner said gloomily, "of inaccuracies." Given Berliner's kindness, he tried to find a delicate way of conveying his disapprobation – but the man, thin-skinned and vain at one and the same time, reacted violently: "You are like all the other American economists! You obviously don't like me!" Convinced that most American Sovietologists criticized his writings out of personal dislike, the man managed to obtain enough money to start his own journal, an achievement that would, as he forthrightly admitted, allow him to publish his own pieces without interference from outsiders. The journal folded after three issues.

Berliner and I agreed that our friend's reaction was classically "Soviet". The tendency to confuse personal with objective criteria, to assume that endorsement denoted affection and disapproval disguised hostility, smacked of the Bolshevik ethos. One of the saddest examples of this I came across in Simon Sebag Montefiore's recent volume on Stalin. Montefiore cites a note discovered on Stalin's night-table after his death. Written by Nikolai Bukharin, one of Stalin's one-time allies and most tragic victims, it reads: "Koba! [Stalin's nickname] Why do you want me dead?"

I remember many other colleagues and contributors with affection and gratitude. For a long time I was on cordial terms with the historian Richard Pipes, but his increasing conservatism made it difficult for us to maintain a smooth relationship. He loathed most of his fellow Sovietologists as garden variety liberals and Soviet apologists who failed to understand that the Soviet Union was not only a species of detestable Leninism, but heir to the Russian "patrimonial" tradition, immanent and unalterable. On one occasion, after I performed some Yiddish songs to a group of people from Harvard University, I mischievously told Pipes that I sang several Yiddish revolutionary songs "just for your sake." Pipes batted no eyelash. "You know,' he said, "I always thought that Russian Jews under the Tsar made a big mistake by joining revolutionary movements: all it did was to create more anti-Semitic feelings among the Russians." I wanted to ask Pipes whether he also thought American blacks should not have rebelled against slavery because this only contributed to the spread of Jim Crow throughout the States, but kept still, smiled, and helped myself to another piece of cake.

On the other hand, though we have had our political disagreements, my friendship with historian Walter Laqueur continues, more than fifty years after it began. In 1954, Laqueur, then living in London, asked me whether I could supply him with the mailing list of our journal's subscribers, inasmuch as he was soon launching a magazine called *Soviet Survey*. His magazine, later renamed *Survey* and from 1965 until its demise thirty years later edited by the historian and sociologist Leo Labedz, turned into a worthy competitor of *POC*. Laqueur, a man of remarkable energy who publishes voluminously – at least one book per year in addition to essays, articles and reviews - has an amazing knowledge of European, especially German, history, and of Israeli politics. (In his youth he belonged for a time to a radical kibbutz.) I have frequently benefited from his help and advice.

I remember fondly Renato Mieli, one-time secretary to the Italian Communist leader, Palmiro Togliatti, and later author of a much-praised biography of his former boss. Elegant, gentle, and soft-spoken, he came to see me in the late 1960s with the suggestion that we let his institute publish an Italian edition of our journal. The idea appealed very much to my superiors, colleagues and myself, and so in two months, a new journal, *Problemas del Communismo*, began to appear in Milan, with the side benefit for me of opportunities to visit Mieli and his wife in their magnificent palazzo on the Grand Canal in Venice. On one such visit, a Sunday afternoon during the 1979 Biennalle that was devoted to dissident art in Eastern Europe, a group of Russian writers suddenly turned up at Mieli's door. Their quite inebriated spokesman, Victor Nekrasov, author of the famous novel *In the Trenches of Stalingrad*, posed a conundrum to Mieli: how, he demanded, could Italy, a country so beautiful, so prosperous, so full of attractive people and wonderful food and drink, tolerate such a large Communist Party? (It was obvious that Nekrasov had not read Carlo Levi's *Christ Stopped at Eboli*, or visited the slums of the south.) Mieli, professorial, patient, fully comprehended the bafflement of his guests: hadn't he, a quintessential Italian, once himself been a fervent believer? With a smile, he explained to his guests how this was not only possible, but perfectly understandable. I don't remember exactly what he said but I recall Nekrasov embracing the Italian. Love at first sight, Russian soul to Italian heart - before the Russians left, as unceremoniously as they had arrived.

Another man to whom I was partial, Alec Nove, ran the Soviet Studies Department at Glasgow University in Scotland. An economist by profession, author of several excellent books, Nove was an eccentric, given to spicing his lectures with bad jokes, and so restless he couldn't stand still for more than a few minutes: waiting with him on a train platform was a trying experience. The son of a Menshevik, he had a profound knowledge of and love for Russian literature, and moreover he continuously tried to find logical reasons for Stalin's most irrational policies. Possessed of a booming voice, he woke everyone, including his long-suffering wife, one winter morning at about half past six when my two children and I, in addition to a number of American Sovietologists, were staying in his cavernous house in Glasgow - by playing a Bach cantata through loudspeakers installed in every single room, while loudly exclaiming, "Friends! *Tovarishchi*! The porridge is ready! Come and get it!" Which family and international guests, all fifteen or so of us, did, gathering in the spacious kitchen to consume the sizzling oatmeal and loudly praise its energetic cook. It was an experience never to be forgotten.

14

Poland Again

*National Culture. Friends, Colleagues. The Eternal Wanderer.
Poles Apart. In the Shadow of Solidarity. Despair and Hope.
The Dissipation of a Dream.*

My professional life, roughly from the mid-1970s on, revolved around the same two countries that dominated my early childhood and youth, Poland and Russia. This was reflected in my work on the journal *Problems of Communism*, in the work I did for the State Department's Office of External Research, and in my non-professional activities.

As a young child I was only dimly aware of my feelings about Poland. Gradually they grew into something I could consciously identify as part love, part abhorrence. Though outrageously at odds with each other, I felt them both with equal intensity: pride in Poland's Romantic history, its splendid literature, its patriots' willingness - according to the National Myth – to lay down their lives for "universal brotherhood and freedom;" rage at the venomous anti-Semitism and intolerance of "the Other" that characterized so much of Polish life. As the Polish sociologist and historian Jerzy Jedlicki puts it, the extreme Polish nationalist's image of the Jew is indestructible. He is "the homeless wanderer, killer of Christ, poisoner, spy, plotter, nabob, usurer, speculator, communist, traitor, bogus convert, and at every twist and turn sworn enemy of the Polish (or for that mattered every other Central European) nation. Without this mythical Jew, ruling the world from his secret lair, the mental landscape of a Polish nationalist - genuine patriot and Catholic, to be sure - cannot be grasped...To this day, many Christians conjure up this image of the Jew to justify violence, vilification, murder, pogroms. The Jew, the eternal schemer, is an irreplaceable fixture; he cannot be killed, because he is immortal."[7]

Jedlicki's portrait of a Polish nationalist may seem to be overdrawn, but it matches my own experiences. As a boy, for instance, I might one day attend a class on Polish literature in which the teacher spoke glowingly of Mickiewicz's Jewish hero, Jankiel the Zither Player, whose rendition of Polish patriotic songs would bring his Polish listeners to tears. A few minutes later, on the way home, I might be – and occasionally was - accosted by a gang of Polish ruffians taunting me with a hail of expletives and an occasional rock. There was nothing about my attire or bearing to remind them of the prime object of their detestation - the chassid with his black caftan, hat (or *shtreyml*) and long ear locks. Rather, though I didn't dress or even look much different from them, I was nevertheless an Alien, the "Eternal Jew," so aptly depicted by Jedlicki.

As I grew older, I grasped more clearly that anti-Semitism was not only an integral part of rooted Polish folk culture, but of Polish politics. Before the war, the most ruthless exponents of the "Jewish danger" were the National Democrats, or "Endeks," organizers of pogroms, boycotts of Jewish stores, and eventually the champions of the need to eliminate Jewish influence from Polish life altogether.[8] Though admirers of the Nazis, few Endeks actually espoused the physical elimination of Jews; still, to this day it remains a mystery how more than three and a half million Jews - about ten percent of the country's pre-war population - could have been "accommodated" abroad so as to decisively eliminate their influence over Polish life. Twenty years after the war, in a bitterly ironic turn of political events, it was the Polish Communists, in the past the only political party free of anti-Semitism, that became the heir to the Endeks' tradition of anti-Jewish hatred. (I had asked Czesław Miłosz to write a piece for *Problems of Communism* on anti-Semitism in the Polish Communist Party; the result, an immensely revealing article, came out in 1957.)

My personal bond to Poland and my sensitivity to its special problems did not ever disappear. On the positive side I retained my passionate interest in various aspects of Polish non- or anti-official thought, the mushrooming of small anti-regime groups, each boasting its own ideological beliefs on a spectrum from democratic nationalist to democratic socialist, and the phenomenal growth of an underground press starting in the late seventies. I understood more and more clearly how the Polish intellectual and political scene differed from those in the other East European countries, in part because of the regime's fairly lenient attitude toward the powerful Catholic Church in return for the Church's tacit obedience to the State. Poland remained a loyal member of the Soviet camp. But it achieved a certain *modus vivendi* with society by making concessions to the Church, by tolerating a relatively critical press - as long as it observed the taboo on criticism of the Soviet Union - and by permitting guarded departures from the canon of "socialist realism" in the arts - that is, a more relaxed censorship.

Over the years I acquired a good number of acquaintances and personal friends, among them the philosopher Leszek Kolakowski, the teacher and political activist Wiktor Kulerski, the journalist Marian Turski (for many years a member of the editorial board of the weekly *Polityka*, Poland's most outspoken weekly), the writer Joanna Wisniewicz, the economist Tadeusz Kowalik and his wife Irena, sociologists Jan Strzelecki and Alina Cała, the feminist critic Bożena Uminska, the journalist and Jewish activist Konstanty Gebert – most of them names unfamiliar to non-Polish readers, but people who represented a wide swath of public opinion and attitudes. They were candid in sharing their views and information with me, and I learned a great deal in the process. Bronisław Geremek, eminent historian and Foreign Minister of Poland in the 1990's, was particularly helpful at a time when he himself was under continuous police surveillance, in the 1980s. I met my new Polish acquaintances in Washington, in London, in Paris and for that matter in Warsaw, which became a regular destination for some years. My own articles on Poland, appearing in *The New York Review of Books, The New York Times, Dissent* and *The New Republic*, drew the attention of the Polish Embassy, some of whose officials began to invite me to lunch and to Embassy parties, sometimes typically stilted diplomatic affairs but often surprisingly informative.

I became so involved in Polish affairs because I still maintained emotional, linguistic and intellectual ties to Poland. My first trip to Poland after the war took place in 1958; I described it in an article in *Commentary* magazine, and for a long time thereafter each subsequent visit aroused childhood recollections of people and places hardly remembered, half buried in my memory. Gradually, however, the memories began to fade, and contemporary Poland claimed my concern. What remained and what principally guided my activities at that time was the determination to understand how Poland, while Communist, nevertheless boasted specific traits distinguishing it from the other "people's democracies" - and to explain them.

This meant, among other things, examining the insidious poison of anti-Semitism. I found it alive and all too thriving even among members of the intelligentsia who firmly denied harboring any anti-Jewish feelings. When I cited chapter and verse, I would often be told that I was exaggerating, and didn't really understand "the general situation." Which meant that I failed to appreciate the historically "objective" reasons for anti-Jewish hostility, such as the large number of Jews residing in Poland before the war (10% of Poland's population), their cultural and religious insularity, and the fact that the Jews found themselves for nearly two centuries in economic competition with the Poles. These reasons "explained" the quest throughout the 1930s for an "extra-territorial" solution for them… The popular slogan *Svój do swego!* (each to his own) no longer resonated as loudly as before the war, but its echo still filled the air: Jews remained the eternal aliens.

One heard, too, embarrassingly meretricious "proof" of how Jewish behavior made life miserable for the Pole. Thus the eminent Polish sociologist Krystyna Kersten, in her book *Poles-Jews-Communism: Anatomy of Half-Truths* (Warsaw, 1992), mentions as all too common the words of a retired man who in 1991 was unable to buy apples in the store because, he claimed, "his monthly retirement check was too small, what with Jews sending all money to Israel." "One can hear such aberrant statements," writes Ms. Kersten, "in

Poland Again 185

a store, in a taxi, in a train, among family members or groups of friends. And what is it, if not an aberration? At a time when our society is confronted by perhaps even more demanding challenges than those it had to cope with in 1918, when the Polish Republic was being born, it is precisely at this time, in a country virtually devoid of minorities, that anti-Jewish obsessions are again raising their heads. The popular imagination is beset by the topic of Jews in the government, Jews in parliament, in the press, television, and who knows where else. Such conversations are held for all intents and purposes in the open. It is a bleak paradox.... Locating traces of the Jew, once hazy or hidden, has turned into a massive search for evidence of machinations committed by the 'Unknown Hand' - in other words by that Other, the sworn Enemy of Poland, disguised but omnipresent..." (p. 174)

I know the position of Jews in Poland has changed considerably in the last few decades. Many Jews, now constituting less than one percent of the population, assert themselves ethnically and religiously. Honest discussions proliferated in the wake of evidence of savage post-war massacres perpetrated by Poles against Jews, evidence unearthed and openly confronted. Matters improved, though not quite on a scale often assumed in the West. Many people in Poland today detest anti-Semitism and xenophobia, and have denounced them time and again, as I noted an essay I wrote for *Foreign Affairs* ("Poland and the Jews," September-October 2002).

But despite all the extraordinary changes in Polish politics and society, many shibboleths retain their unfortunate hold on the popular imagination. At the very time when Poles were emerging from limbo, when the garroting censorship disappeared and it became possible to write openly and honestly on subjects that had been either taboo or deliberately distorted, just when a sense of vast relief and confidence should have prevailed, it had to contend with the old noxious mixture of fear, bigotry and myth-making. The Jews were no longer there. But The Jew remained. The image of the guileful, cunning, pitiless Stranger, far from vanishing, if anything gained prominence. I found the phenomenon mind-boggling as well as disheartening.

One trivial but revealing illustration: during a long ride in a taxicab from one end of Warsaw to the other, my driver and I began to chat. We had plenty of time. This was during the Martial Law period, imposed by General Jaruzelski after outlawing Solidarity in early 1982. Did you belong to Solidarity? I asked the driver. "Oh, yes," he answered cheerfully. "And how was it?" I continued. My driver, whose accent suggested peasant origins, became animated. "It was terrific!" he said. "You know, we all had little flags (*choragewki*) and waved them wherever we went. There was only one problem," he lowered his voice. "It was them." "Them? Who?" "Oh, the *żydki* (Jew-boys)," he replied. "They were everywhere." "Everywhere?" I said, puzzled. "Surely you don't mean that Lech Walesa is Jewish?" He giggled. "Oh, no, of course not. But believe me, sir, they were everywhere, everywhere." We arrived at our destination. I gave him a large tip, shook his hand and said: "Thank you for an interesting conversation, One thing I want to tell you - I am Jewish. Good-bye." He stood there, in something of a daze. Which is how I left him.

The drama that engulfed Poland in the 1980s was played out against the background of the Solidarity movement, which began as a series of sporadic strikes in the summer of 1980 and then snowballed into a national trade union first in the shipyards of Gdansk, and then in other industrial centers and social groups, eventually penetrating most public bodies. For a time, Poland looked like a powder keg waiting to explode. Disastrous government economic policies had created massive impoverishment and discontent. Poland's history of insurrections, large-scale and small, a history of which the Soviets were well aware and the Polish rulers more so, may well have stayed the hands of those itching to apply the Hungarian or Czech scenarios in Warsaw; no one wanted a military confrontation. The Polish government embarked on a policy of negotiations with Solidarity, which in the meantime was gathering strength, attracting to its ranks a number of seasoned Polish intellectuals in the role of political consultants. Such parleys, initiated by the government from a position of weakness, were bound to redound to the advantage - at least in the short run - of the regime's adversaries.

At the same time, the Polish government, anxious not to provoke the Soviets, spread rumors that it was under enormous pressure to "request" Soviet assistance, the usual Soviet formula to justify its "help" in crushing a "common enemy," and that Solidarity needed to show its patriotism by making concessions to the government. Myself, I was convinced that the Soviets would do almost anything to avoid an armed clash: Poland's forces were the second largest in Eastern Europe, and Polish anti-Soviet animus lurked barely below the surface. To embark on a military path was playing with fire. Many Soviet and East European specialists, in and out of government, disagreed. On the other hand, many, including some of the leaders of and advisors to Solidarity, thought that Solidarity had dangerously overestimated its strength and was heedlessly provoking the government by accelerating its demands.

Whether General Jaruzelski proclaimed martial law in December 1981 in order to avoid a Soviet invasion - as he has maintained consistently since then - still remains an open question. Some of Solidarity's leaders, who were then certain that the government was using the Soviet threat as an elaborate ruse, have subsequently changed their minds. One of the more curious cases has been the amicable relationship that has developed between the General and Adam Michnik, once one of Poland's most prominent dissidents and now editor of the country's largest newspaper, *Gazeta wyborcza*. No one has been able to explain it to me altogether satisfactorily. Politics makes for strange bedfellows indeed, and the recent past still shadows the country, especially with the revelations made possible with the opening of the archives of the secret police. Every few months or so, a new scandal erupts. People open their morning newspaper to find their names listed as former collaborators of the security services; weeks of accusations and counter-accusations follow, reputations fall, others rise, thus helping to poison the political atmosphere of the country.

Thinking back to Solidarity's emergence and its early, "heroic" period, my response strikes me as very much of a piece with my reaction to the 1956 Hungarian uprising and the Prague Spring of 1968 in Czechoslovakia. All three cases fanned the hope that perhaps now we could finally see the beginning of the end of communism. The Hungarian Revolution, the Czechoslovak "socialism with a human face" and Solidarity all seemed harbingers of a process that might, in time, change the political landscape of Eastern Europe. My own experiences with Soviet reality notwithstanding, I yielded, as Marxists might say, to the illusions of a "false consciousness."

This held especially true for Poland. My old ambivalence resurfaced, this time bifurcated between enthusiasm for Solidarity and profound disquiet - to put it mildly - about the depth of anti-Semitic feelings in Poland, excitement about what was frequently referred to as the country's *odnowa* (renewal) on the one hand, despair over obdurate anti-Jewish feelings on the other. I myself found most exciting the reaction of the rank-and-file of the Communist Party to the "renewal." Not only did members leave in droves (several hundred thousand by December 1980), but within the party pro-Solidarity sympathy was growing, and several reformist movements emerged. Their reforms boiled down to eliminating centralization, which imposed discipline on party members from above, and replacing it with the "horizontal principle" which advocated complete equality within the party's basic organization.. According to this concept, the majority's will, democratically expressed, should dictate the leadership's decisions. It meant no more and no less than abolishing the Leninist principle of "democratic centralism" (i.e., the center decides, the party loyally - "democratically" - falls into line) - the essence of the Communist system. Not surprisingly, the espousal of democratic processes intoxicated many party members: after all, it was tantamount to demanding that power be wrested away from the autocratic and self-aggrandizing bureaucracy, and be placed in true proletarian hands. To well-wishers abroad, the demands promised seismic changes in the very nature of communist rule.

Many of Solidarity's expectations turned out to be misguided, inflated, or just plain wrong. The Catholic Church, for instance, notwithstanding the convictions of many Poles, did not really turn into a partisan of Solidarity, though individual priests became known for their Solidarity sympathies. Rather, it continued to maneuver between loyalty to the government - which dismayed many believers - and sympathy for Solidarity, which aroused the hostility of its (in effect) Communist partner in power. Add to this that hundreds of thousands of Solidarity members deserted their organization soon after martial law was declared, in December 1981, and it is clear that organization's boastful claims of overwhelming support (roughly ten million members, supposedly) had been spawned by wishful thinking.

Similarly, the adulation of Lech Wałesa, so overwhelming at first, also moderated. In the summer of 1981, I interviewed Wałesa in Gdansk for about two hours. They were two wretched hours: Wałesa proved vain, crude, simplistic, and devoid entirely of the charm so frequently ascribed to him. He had obviously been the man of the hour in the summer and autumn of 1980. Less than a year later, he was beginning to display all the traits of a pampered child. I remember his visit to Washington several years after that, accompanied by an affable young man, a Solidarity activist. On the evening of the second day, he spoke with a small group of local admirers of Solidarity, myself included. He was in despair. What happened? That afternoon, he told us, he and Wałesa met with a few people and Wałesa, feeling altogether at home, let loose with a few of the usual epithets about the *żydki*, the *żydokomuna* - nothing unusual, mind you, just the local *gwara* (patois) common among friends. The man tried (vainly) to remonstrate with Walesa, if only on grounds of the impolitic nature of his comments. "Can you imagine," he asked us, "what will happen to us when Wałesa's language becomes known?" Fortunately for Wałesa and Solidarity, Western popular enthusiasm for Poland was so fierce that incidents like this one - and others, some much worse - were passed over in silence.

Nevertheless, I do not regret my hopefulness, nor do I think it was it entirely misplaced. Despite the persistence of anti-Semitism, the small Jewish community in Poland has experienced a remarkable rebirth, creating a functioning synagogue, a fine monthly journal, courses in Hebrew and Yiddish, and above all a sense of empowerment that the Jewish community in Poland had never before enjoyed. Right-wing nationalistic ideology, often in tandem with Catholic groups and institutions (such as Radio Marija, presided over by a rabble-rousing anti-Semitic priest), survives, with a sturdy presence in the parliament (Sejm). Yet the latter, under Communist rule little more than a rubber-stamping tool, has become a genuinely representative body. Economically the country, its elite strongly influenced by extreme Western market-economy ideas, has fared poorly, with high unemployment and wage inequality, but at the same time the country's strong commitment to democratic values provides hope for change and progress. For me personally, although I still have close friends in Poland, the country itself has become something of a distant relation. The bond remains, but it has become attenuated, somehow painful and rusty at the edges.

15

Russia Again

The Priviligentsia... Workers versus Workers? Dissent and Samizdat. A soupçon of liberalism. Shifting Patterns. Three Portraits.

The unrest that swept the Soviet imperium after Stalin's death first hit the peripheries, the territories in Eastern Europe that fell to Soviet control during and after World War II. But the tremors that spread through the interior USSR, while not as dramatically visible as in Eastern Europe, were no less significant.

The first to voice their discontent were the intelligentsia, more specifically the "creative intelligentsia" – the writers and artists, the men and women called upon to portray the iniquities of the capitalist system, and above all the road, arduous but inspiring, to the "radiant future."

The result of this mandate was the production of mountains of lusterless drivel, for magazines, books, the screen, the stage. Their authors, the masters of "socialist realism", enjoyed status just below that of the party *nomenklatura* (officialdom), the most pampered class in Soviet society. They earned huge royalties, got access to large apartments, dachas, even occasionally enjoyed that most coveted of Soviet awards - a trip abroad.

Then something extraordinary happened. In July 1962, in the industrial town of Novocherkassk, south of Moscow, several hundred workers from a locomotive factory laid down their tools and took to the streets. Joined by several thousand others, they marched carrying portraits of Lenin, flowers, and banners. They demanded higher wages and the reversal of the increases in the food prices just announced by the authorities. After a taut stand-off, the militia fired into the crowd, and the local hospitals were soon filled with dead and wounded. A trial followed, the usual rigged affair: confessions of crimes never committed, "spontaneous" meetings of workers demanding "justice" for the criminals, and so on. Some of the accused were sentenced to death, a few to long prison terms.[9]

A strike by workers in the "workers' state?" Soon it turned out that the eruption in Novocherkassk was not an isolated event, though other strikes and protests were smaller in scale. Most of them had been triggered by the harsh economic policies which some in the party leadership warned against and which galvanized the workers into voicing standard working class demands not heard in the Soviet Union for decades: higher wages, lower prices, better working conditions, and negotiations between management and workers, the last one most noteworthy, given the standard Soviet rhetoric about the team of management and labor, peacefully united in their common aim of building socialism.

Many members of the *priviligentsia*, while favored by the regime, in fact led lives of quiet desperation. Some were corrupt enough not to care whether the rubbish expected of them daily was true or not. Others closed their eyes. If forced to attend a meeting to approve the obloquy thrown upon somebody presumably guilty of some offense against "socialist realism", they attended, and approved: perhaps they might thus avoid their own turn at a humiliating act of public self-criticism?

But there were also among the *priviligentsia* those who tried to keep their collaboration with the authorities at a minimum. They consigned some of their works "to the drawer," that is, their own personal files, and they waited. Gradually, these writers (the "liberals") were able to voice some of their heterodox views more openly in the official journals, especially in the journal *Novyi mir* (The New World), edited from the late 1950s until 1970 by the popular and relatively outspoken poet Alexander Tvardovski. Conservatives, closet Stalinists, anti-Semites or neo-Slavophiles (right-wing nationalists) also found a niche, and thus protection in one or another of the official journals sympathetic to their views.

To observers abroad, the most sympathetic group in this diverse literary-political scene that developed in the Soviet Union from the early 1960s on were the oppositional liberal writers and artists, or as they began to be called, the "dissidents." Some wore their dissidence proudly, a badge proclaiming their defiance of official values, and the authorities retaliated, either by way of press attacks, or in some cases by arrest and exile. They circulated their work unofficially, via handwritten or typed copies. Many of these *samizdat* (self-published, i.e. uncensored) texts had little artistic or even political merit, but they were all authentic, a genuinely alternative literature.

In *Problems of Communism*, we published excerpts from and discussion of some of the *samizdat* literature, and in 1968, we put out a special issue of the journal devoted entirely to this subject. I published the material, along with supplementary texts, as a book, *In Quest Of Justice - Protest and Dissent in the Soviet Union Today*. Thus we revealed a reality hardly known to Western readers, the existence of a small but surprisingly influential group of liberals straining at the leash of a detested dictatorship. Their "crimes" were not political in any activist sense of the word. They struggled for breathing space, for the right to portray their lives objectively and truthfully, to express sadness when sadness was called for instead of spurious optimism.

In the early 1970s, the Soviet authorities decided that a policy of controlled concessions would be preferable to one of punitive measures alone. They didn't rule out arrest and banishment, but gave more dissidents a chance to depart from the Soviet Union, usually in a matter of days or at most weeks. For some of them, emigration in such circumstances amounted to forced exile; others eagerly accepted the chance to "choose freedom," as the title of a well-known book by a KGB escapee from Stalin's Russia, Victor Kravchenko, had it. I had taken a leave of absence from USIA in 1971 and accepted a fellowship at the London School of Economic and Political Science (LSE) to do some research on dissent and *samizdat* in the Soviet Union. Immediately I was sucked into the group of people working on Soviet dissent - academics, journalists, artists – mainly under the aegis of Peter Reddaway, of the Political Science Department at LSE, a man of considerable energy and dedication. He was known for his belief that "our dissidents" were destined one of these days to become the leaders of Russia, a slightly romantic notion that many of us esteemed but did not necessarily share. Nonetheless, we developed close bonds with the émigrés, taking up their cause (or causes, since the dissidents were split along various ideological and tactical lines) in newspaper articles, radio programs and occasional conferences held under the sponsorship of LSE and other educational institutions, and maintaining contact with those still in the Soviet Union.

Some of the many people I met during my tenure as editor of *Problems of Communism* and for a few years thereafter made a profound impression on me, conjuring up to this day images of meetings in Moscow and elsewhere. One extremely striking figure whom I met in the mid-1970s was Andrei Amalrik, a gifted essayist and historian. In his late thirties when I met him, he had refused to yield to Soviet pressure, and had sent forceful essays abroad for publication. He felt strongly on all subjects, including the stupidity of the Soviet authorities and the cowardice of Western correspondents who avoided meeting with Soviet dissidents in Moscow for fear of earning the displeasure of the Soviet regime. This was an attitude which Amalrik, a proud man, could justifiably claim never to have succumbed to himself. In 1969 he wrote a remarkably prescient essay, "Will the Soviet Union Survive Until 1984?" where he foresaw a break between Communist China and the Soviet Union.

I liked both the boyish Amalrik, with his dry sense of humor, and his captivating wife Gyuzel, a Crimean Tatar and an accomplished "unofficial" painter. When Amalrik came to the States on a fellowship in 1977 or 1978, I invited them to stay at our house in the Washington suburbs until they could find a place for themselves. They accepted, and I discovered that Amalrik's stubborn pride - entertaining in small doses – easily slipped into rather tiresome narcissism after a while. "*Ya liubliu narod i narod menya liubit*" (I love the people and the people love me), he was fond of saying occasionally, ironically quoting one of Stalin's favorite *bon mots* but applying it seriously to himself.

One evening, I arranged a reception for the Amalriks, held at a splendid mansion in southern Maryland, where they could meet a sprinkling of Washington's *nomenklatura* as well as intellectuals with an interest in Soviet affairs. Amalrik enjoyed himself hugely, and the following morning, I expected the guest of honor to say a few words of appreciation. Instead, at the breakfast table, he looked at me sourly and said "You know, Abe, it occurs to me that you are really doing very little for me and my fellow dissidents." For a moment, I was taken aback, but then recalled what my father used to say to me, in Yiddish, when I was a little boy and made what he thought were exorbitant demands: *"vos vilstu nokh, mayn zun, dos telerl fun himl?"* (what else do you need, my son, the saucer from the sky?). I translated these words to Amalrik, who looked at me quizzically and said nothing. The subject never came up between us again. A few years later, Amalrik died in a car accident in Spain; Gyuzel remarried and disappeared, at least from the Soviet émigré world.

A fairly frequent companion of mine in those years was Victor Zorza, the Soviet specialist of *The Manchester Guardian* in London. Zorza, in his middle forties when I knew him, was a short man with a round head and prominent cheeks, always tense and unable to talk about anything, as far as I could tell, except the Soviet Union. Born somewhere in Galicia, he found himself deported by Soviet troops to Kazakhstan in 1941. Two years later, desperate to leave his place of banishment, he embarked on an arduous trip by railroad to Moscow, where he was determined to meet the journalist Ilya Ehrenburg. He thought Ehrenburg could help him join the Polish army that was being formed under Soviet aegis in Moscow. Zorza had never met Ehrenburg, whom he admired as a writer, but he somehow managed a meeting, where his determination and insouciance so impressed the Soviet writer that Ehrenburg immediately made two or three phone calls which opened the gates of the Kosciuszko Infantry Division to the young man, and sent him off to the Eastern front.

How, within two years of the war's end, Zorza got himself to London and persuaded the editor of *The Manchester Guardian* to give him a job on the newspaper's Soviet desk is another remarkable story, testimony to Zorza's strength of will, his eloquence and also his intimate knowledge of the Soviet Union. Within a relatively brief span, Zorza's industriousness and perspicacity won him a respectable niche in the newspaper's editorial establishment; his success enabled him to move himself and all his paraphernalia into a house about twenty miles from London, which became his residence cum headquarters, with the somewhat dazed compliance of the paper's editor. There Zorza would walk around in jeans and torn sweater, showing off his keep, rather on the shabby side, but all of it his, from top to bottom. His English wife, by profession a nurse, would cook almost all the meals, often assisted by their teen-aged daughter.

Given his achievements, it was not altogether surprising that Zorza, otherwise a gentle man, was consumed by a powerful ego. Thus he didn't find anything irregular in phoning at any hour of day or night (we were all, as it were, his informants...) to locate a certain Soviet provincial newspaper that Zorza "desperately" needed. I was a frequent recipient of such phone requests, though I could hardly ever satisfy him, except by referring him to someone else.

Zorza was the single most gifted exponent of the "Kremlinological" school of Soviet affairs, which explained almost all Soviet policies in terms of a continual struggle for power among the member of the ruling elite. The fact that his friends could not always help him to locate a crucial piece of evidence - and Zorza was a stickler for evidence - showed that assurances notwithstanding, they did not really stand by him and his concepts. One early evening, on a walk through Hampstead Heath, he suddenly asked me, "Abe, do you think you could use your good offices to get me a medal from the Department of State?" My bafflement (my "good offices!") was then matched by his: "Is it so difficult to imagine why I deserve a medal for all my work in successfully explaining and predicting Soviet behavior?" he wondered aloud. Zorza was particularly aggrieved that he had not been recognized as one of the few Sovietologists to have foreseen the Soviet invasion of Czechoslovakia in

1968. And perhaps he should have been. But there was something ineffably naïve (and egotistic) about hoping to be awarded a medal (!) from the State Department for his efforts.

Many years later Zorza's daughter fell ill with a terminal disease, and her doctors recommended hospice care, then a relatively new and decidedly under-funded phenomenon. The care she received was outstanding, and Zorza so admired the idea of hospices that he quit his job and spent several years, together with his wife, raising money for a special hospice organization. His will remained indomitable. After his daughter died - "very peacefully," he said - he did not resume his previous job at *The Guardian*, but persuaded the editors of *The London Times* to send him to a small hamlet in North India. From there he sent weekly dispatches to the paper describing the life of the villagers, impoverished but filled, as Zorza put it, with "quiet heroism." If the subject was new for Zorza, the intensity of his involvement and the intelligence he brought to bear were not, and his dispatches were typically engrossing and astute. He died shortly thereafter.

The man who was so instrumental in launching Victor Zorza's literary career, Ilya Ehrenburg, was someone I, too, had long admired - indeed, ever since adolescence, when I read his collection of short stories called *The Thirteen Pipes*. One story that made a shattering impression on me described the Christmas truce of World War I: how during the night of December 24, 1914 the guns along the trenches on the Western front fell silent, and from both sides unshaven and bedraggled British and German soldiers appeared, toasting one another and singing "Silent Night;" they even played impromptu soccer games. Sadly, within days the carnage resumed, with the same soldiers who exchanged cigarettes only a night or two before now back in the daily business of shooting each others' brains out.

Ehrenburg published *The Thirteen Pipes* early in his career, and his cynicism was as acrid as his sentimentality was poignant, both qualities displayed in his book. This combination, not unusual in a writer of romantic inclinations, marked his other books, too, almost all of them novels. Throughout the 1920s and '30s, Ehrenburg lived off and on in Paris, where he became a close friend of the artistic avant-garde; many of his friends, poets and painters like Chagall and Braque, gave him some of their work as tokens of respect and personal friendship.

Ehrenburg was as ambidextrous politically as he was aesthetically, at once a quintessentially liberal and open-minded European writer and critic and a committed Communist. Moreover, his communism was not of the left-bank variety, but testified to an earnest commitment to the Soviet Union. Just before the war broke out, he returned to Moscow from Paris, continuing to write both belles-lettres and journalism. Covering the war as an eyewitness correspondent for the Army's newspaper, *Krasnaya zvezda* (Red Star), he gained fame with his chilling accounts of Nazi barbarities. Though himself a wholly secular, non-practicing Jew, Ehrenburg emphasized his Jewish identity in response to the Nazi anti-Semitic slaughter; eventually he and the Soviet Jewish writer Vasili Grossman became engaged in a project to publish a full account of Nazi atrocities. A month after the German attack on the Soviet Union, Ehrenburg declared: "I grew up in a Russian city. My native language is Russian, I am a Russian writer. I am defending my homeland. But the Nazis have reminded me of something else: my mother's name was Hannah. I am a Jew. I say this with pride. Hitler hates us more than anyone else. And that does us credit."[10]

After Stalin's death Ehrenburg began to publish volumes of criticism and memoirs clearly designed to counter the effect on young Soviet readers of years of meretricious writings about Soviet literature and Soviet cultural life in general. He managed to get stories by Isaac Babel, murdered in 1937, back into print; he supported Pasternak. His writings found a grateful response from readers. In addition, in 1954 Ehrenburg published a thin novel called *The Thaw*, which included references to the notorious Doctors' Plot and the poison of Stalin's anti-Jewish ("anti-cosmopolitan") campaign, and which lent its name to the hopeful, spring-like atmosphere that prevailed after Stalin's demise. A few years later, he wrote "The Lessons of Stendhal," an essay in which Stendhal's remarks about tyranny served as a way of protesting the reimposition of conformity and literary censorship.

In 1961, I came on one of my occasional trips to Moscow. This was the year when Ehrenburg celebrated his 70th birthday in grand style; he took the opportunity of a speech at the Writers' Union gala to rebut Stalin's characterization of writers as "engineers of the human soul," calling them instead "teachers of life." Could I meet him, I asked my Soviet friends. To my pleasant surprise, help came from an unexpected source - Galina, a young woman in her late twenties whom I had met in Moscow two years earlier, a knowledgeable guide at the Hermitage Museum in Leningrad and also a guide for the Soviet tourist agency Intourist. "What would you most like to do in Moscow?" Galina asked, when we met at the Ukraina Hotel. "Meet Ilya Ehrenburg," I replied. "He has been something of a hero of mine." Before I knew it, she opened her special Intourist address book and got on the phone to the writer. It was an impressive performance. "This is the Moscow office of Intourist," she said calmly (this on the hotel phone!). "We have a guest here, an American, a well-known writer and journalist, and a great admirer of yours, who would love to see you." "Well," said Ehrenburg (as she subsequently informed me), "I am a busy man. I am about to depart for Rome tomorrow. Can't we do it some other time?" "I am about to depart for Rome"! It was not often that you heard such words in Moscow in those days... But Galina persisted. "Couldn't you possibly see him this afternoon," she asked, "if only for an hour? He is returning to America tomorrow. He would be most grateful." Ehrenburg finally relented, and an hour later we were ringing the doorbell of his flat on Gorky Street (now Tverskaya), four blocks away from revolutionary Red Square in a house obviously occupied by members of the *nomenklatura*.

A winsome woman opened the door; I recognized her from photographs as Ehrenburg's wife. Smiling silently, she led us immediately into her husband's study, dominated by a large desk on which stood a bottle of dry vermouth - again, not a common sight in the land of the Soviets.... And near the desk stood Ehrenburg himself.

His appearance took me aback. He was slight, looked older than his seventy years, had a deeply furrowed face and crooked, nicotine-discolored front teeth. When he started speaking, however, you forgot about his appearance. He was a riveting conversationalist.

I had brought along a recent issue of *Problems of Communism* to present to Ehrenburg. It carried about a dozen poems, in Russian and in translation, by an anonymous author, which we had entitled

"Poems from the Underground," and published together with a commentary by the (equally anonymous) translator. We merely identified him as a well-known poet whose works also appear in open Soviet publications (which was true). Ehrenburg took one look at the poems, and said matter of factly: "I see you published poems by Boris Slutsky." "I don't know who the author is," I replied, "but we thought the poems would be of considerable potential interest to our readers." "But yours is a political journal, isn't it?" continued Ehrenburg, while leafing through the magazine. "Why this interest in poetry?" I explained that we were indeed a political journal, but we were also curious about literary and cultural subjects, especially those with important political implications. "We all walked under god," read one verse. And another:

> I recall the frowning Germans, the sad prisoners of 1945 at interrogation.
> I ask; they answer. Do you believe in Hitler? No, I don't believe.
> You believe Goering? No, I don't believe.
> You believe Goebbels? Oh, propaganda!
> And do you believe me? A moment of silence.
> Mr. Commissar, I don't believe you.
> Everything is propaganda. The whole world is propaganda.

These lines may not reflect the lyrical quality of Slutsky's verse, but of their political import there could be no doubt.

Soon Ehrenburg was engaged in a spirited conversation with Galina. He led us to another room, where he opened the door to a large closet and started pulling out one canvas after another: Kandinsky, Malevich, Chagall, Picasso, Cezanne... I was getting more and more excited, my companion - a guide to the Hermitage, after all - even more so. Ehrenburg stood calmly, watching our reactions. It was an extraordinary moment. Ehrenburg directed most of his remarks to Galina, not so much, I felt, because she was an attractive young woman as because she represented the generation Ehrenburg was so desperate to reach with his memoirs and literary reminiscences. At one point, I interrupted to ask whether

Ehrenburg maintained relations with the few surviving Yiddish writers he had once known so well. "There is Samuel Halkin," he said, "a fine poet, whom I see from time to time... " (He was right: Halkin, a fine lyrical poet, somehow succeeded in avoiding Stalin's axe.) "As for the others..." - he shrugged his shoulders. There was nothing to say after that; we went back to the paintings. Playing the naïve journalist, I asked another question: "Why do you think, Ilya Grigorevich, that the government in the late 1920s simply consigned the Braques, Maleviches and others to limbo? What was the reason for it?"

The reply was pure Ehrenburg: "No doubt you and your colleagues are convinced that there were political reasons for it. Well, my young friend, it will interest you to know that those who rebelled against these modernists were average people - the *prostoy narod*. In the early 1920s some of our excitable young artists, the 'Constructivists,' descended upon Moscow and Leningrad, painting circles and squares on every empty piece of wall. In response, citizens came out with buckets of whitewash and brushes, determined to erase the ugly daubs from their buildings. The party and government decrees," he added with a light smile, "all came afterwards."

Ehrenburg, for all his irony, had a legitimate point. I asked him whether he would mind autographing one of his books. He autographed his volume "On Rereading Chekhov" for Galina, and then took out another copy and scribbled something hurriedly on its title page before handing it to me. We all shook hands, and we also managed to say good-bye to Mrs. Ehrenburg, who appeared once more, leading us to the exit. Back in the hotel, we examined carefully Ehrenburg's scrawl. It said: "To a young American who will yet come to grief for his interest in politics. Ilya Ehrenburg."

16

Envoi

The reader of these pages will have realized by now that the Soviet system and its attendant discipline, Sovietology, filled my adult life, professionally and personally. Even though I had formally retired from the U.S. government before Gorbachev came to power, I continued to follow developments with great interest for several years. Yet the Soviet cum Sovietological worlds were worlds I came to as an adult, albeit a young adult. The formative worlds of my childhood and adolescence, worlds that in many ways set the stage for my adult activities, embraced the world of Yiddish and its secular Jewish culture, and the world of democratic socialism in which I grew up and to which I returned, this time without my early naïve notions, as an adult. Indeed, democratic socialism seems to me now, as I examine my travels, the glue that held my various worlds together, whether visibly or not.

What linked the young boy who told his father that he was already "class conscious" and the young man who presided over the "Yiddish Youth Federation" in the late l940s? What inspired me to write love verses in Yiddish when I was sixteen, and more serious poetry several years on? And what impelled me later to produced a record of Yiddish folk songs, called *Of Lovers, Dreamers, and Thieves*, and several years later a CD on which I recite Yiddish poetry in English and Yiddish? Was there a connection between these activities and the beliefs I imbued as a child? Or between those beliefs and my interest in the growth of Soviet dissidence? Or with my enthusiasm for the Czech "socialism with a human face?" Or my immersion in the ideology and activities of Polish dissent and later the Solidarity movement?

To ask these questions is almost to answer them. Some readers of this memoir may wonder why I devoted so much attention to the role of Yiddish in my childhood: the poems we read, the songs we sang. Yet it is precisely this language, and precisely the values communicated to me in it and by it, that formed my basic attitudes to the world around me. The words from the Medem Sanatorium song "We Are Coming" ("we fashion water out of stone") still resonate with me to this day. I don't think that at the age of nine I believed in our ability to transubstantiate water from stone. But "socialism" carried the promise that, in the words of the *Internationale*, we shall "destroy an evil world" and in its place erect a new, just, equitable one, a goal as attainable as the metamorphosis of stone into water, but far more inspiring. You need not subscribe to transcendental verities to accept that superb confidence can produce miraculous results.

In the more than five decades that elapsed between the demise of Joseph Stalin and the demise of almost the entire edifice of international communism, the world was periodically rocked by tremors that seemed to accelerate - at least in the eyes of many of us - the process of communism's liquidation. Each such phenomenon, slow to appear at first, but gathering force over time, offered the possibility of meaningful change. *Samizdat* was one: it took some time for a society schooled to believe that dissent of any form equaled treason to circulate, at first on the sly, gradually more openly, letters of protest against arrests, trials, and other forms of governmental repression. At first letters were signed by individuals, but in time collective letters of protest proliferated, with the names and addressed of the signatories clearly spelled out. Serious discussions of Soviet law, political essays, history and literature became increasingly common.

What was our reaction to this growing challenge to the regime, for this is indeed what *samizdat* amounted to? For me, it inspired hope that indeed the Soviet system was being undermined from within. *Samizdat* was almost entirely an intelligentsia phenomenon, its authors mainly drawn from the liberal wing who supported Western democratic values. (Right-wing nationalists circulated uncensored texts as well, but to a much smaller extent.) I and many of my colleagues believed that these and not the epigones of Stalin were the people who held the key to the future of the country. I believed so in part because I wanted to believe so, and my desire unquestionably had roots in the values dear to me since childhood.

The title of this book is **Journeys Through Vanishing Worlds**. Since many of these worlds, as I pointed out, were fashioned by optimism and our confidence that they were achievable, why the gloomy term "vanishing?" Foremost, because of the Holocaust, which destroyed my childhood's Poland, the Eastern Europe we tried to cross in fleeing the advancing German armies, the Vilna I knew, the culture it embodied. Some of those worlds vanished without a trace. Others may have disappeared physically, yet their ideas – and ideals - left ineradicable residues. The Medem Sanatorium and the Bundist organizations of my youth fuelled my own resistance, in Vilna and later in the Bronx, to my mates' blindly enthusiastic welcome of the "wave of the future." The Bund's internationalist vision informed my own abhorrence – however ill-directed – of American parochialism. My family's wartime journey across the Soviet Union and my father's tolerant openness toward other ways of life engendered some, at least, of my own curiosity about Russia and its culture. The proud Jewish definition of my upbringing propelled my dogged efforts to arrange a memorial meeting for the victims of the Warsaw Ghetto Uprising. I could go on.

As I look at the various worlds that comprise my lifelong journey, I realize how interdependent they are - the Jewish with the Polish, the European with the American, the cultural with the political, the intellectual with the personal. Each represents part of a hope waiting to be realized, each rests upon institutions, libraries, conversations and histories from which successive generations can continue to learn as they have in the past. Remembering is one way – my way – of contributing to that chain of knowledge, one way of explaining the tensions that forged my own complicated identity and that of many like me, and one way of retaining what I found most compelling in those worlds that are gone. Gone, but alive in memory, and alive in the obduracy of hope. Thus, happily, "vanishing," but not "vanished."

Notes

[1] For an enlightening survey of the Jewish school system in pre-war Poland, see Ezra Mendelsohn, *The Jews of East Central Europe between the Wars* (Bloomington, In.: Indiana Univ. Press, 1983), pp.62-68.

[2] See *Flight and Rescue*. The US Holocaust Commission (Washington, DC: 2001).

[3] Aside from their traditional antipathy for the Jews, and the firm conviction that all Jews were by nature cowardly and spineless (a widespread assumption that tended to be revised by Poles beaten up by Jewish thugs or by "self-defense units", organized by Jewish socialists in the 1930s), the Polish political and military authorities also assumed that the Jewish Fighting Organization, or JFO, was a loyal tool of Moscow. Communists did constitute one of the groups in the JFO; another, the socialist-Zionist Hashomer Hatzair, harbored some pro-Soviet sympathies, and though many others did not, this sufficed to brand the entire Jewish resistance movement a "Communist plot." The strength of this myth contributed to the tragic denouement of the uprising. Even with more weapons, the revolt would have gone down in defeat (as did the Warsaw Polish Uprising one year later), but at least more Germans would have paid for it with their lives, and more Jewish resistance fighters would have died as they wanted to die, with honor.

[4] Henryk Erlich and Wiktor Alter were two of the most outstanding leaders of the Jewish socialist Bund. In October 1939, the two were arrested by the Soviet secret police and charged with espionage on behalf of the Western powers. In the autumn of 1941, shortly after the Germans invaded the USSR, the two Bundists were released in a gesture aimed at pacifying public opinion in the West, and possibly to head what later came to be known as the Jewish Anti-Fascist Committee, designed specifically to seek international Jewish support for the Soviet war effort. Then Stalin changed his mind. The two Bund leaders were rearrested, this time as "German agents." For a long time the Soviets refused to disclose what actually

happened to the two men. Indeed, only after the collapse of the USSR did their fate became known: Erlich, broken by months of cruel interrogation, committed suicide at the Butyrki prison in Moscow; Alter was felled by a bullet at the back of his neck.

[5] Cited by Jeffrey Brooks in *Thank you, Comrade Stalin!* (Princeton: Princeton Univ. Press, 2000), p.109.

[6] *The Operational Code* (New York: McGraw Hill, 1951), p. 47.

[7] "Wiedza jako źr dło cierpień", (Knowledge as the Source of Suffering), *Tygodnik powszechny* (Krakow, Jan. 2005).

[8] Emanuel Melzer, *No Way Out: The Politics of Polish Jewry 1935-1939* (Cincinnati, Oh.: Hebrew Union College Press, 1997).

[9] Samuel H. Baron, *Bloody Saturday in the Soviet Union: Novocherkassk 1962* (Stanford: Stanford Univ. Press, 2001).

[10] Cited by Yuri Slezkine, *The Jewish Century* (Princeton: Princeton Univ. Press, 2005), p. 288.

Printed in the United States
100619LV00003B/91-114/A